Journey Through
DEPLOYMENT

Stepping Forward with Confidence
During Military Separations

Kathryn Sneed

Journey Through Deployment
Stepping Forward with Confidence
During Military Separations

ISBN:
Print   978-0-9911267-3-6

Contact the publisher and author at: SingingThroughTheRain@gmail.com

Credits:

Cover Design: Alane Pearce, Publishing Coach
alane@MyPublishingCoach.com

Cover Photo: Ashley Robinson Photography Facebook.com/
AshleyRobinsonPhotography

Book Layout and Design: Alane Pearce Publishing Coach
alane@MyPublishingCoach.com

Publishing coaching, and project management by Alane Pearce, Professional Writing Services, LLC. For more information, contact Alane at www.MyPublishingCoach.com or email
alane@MyPublishingCoach.com

Sneed, Kathryn: Journey Through Deployment: Stepping Forward with Confidence During Military Separations

1. Self Help   2. Inspirational   3. Military

Contributors:

Sara Horn,
Author of *Weekend Warrior No More*
Excerpt Used With Permission
Contact: SaraHorn.com

A Military Wife's Promise
Written by: Megan Kratochvil Williams
© 2011, All Rights Reserved
Used With Permission.
Contact: ToLoveASoldier.blogspot.com

Aprille Donaldson
Chapters and Excerpts Used With Permission.
Contact: BeautifulInHisTime.com

Acknowledgements

I will never forget standing in Michelle Russell's driveway only a few days after my husband left for his first deployment. I had tears in my eyes as she encouraged me and made me believe that I would get through this deployment no matter what and that she would be there for me.

Michelle, I can never thank you enough for all you did during that deployment. Standing by me and helping me through gave me the confidence I needed to get through those long seven months and made me into the person I am today. Through your encouragement and help I was able to write so many of the blog posts that are now in this book. Thank you for being such a blessing to my life.

Aprille, without you this book would not exist. Although we have never met in person, you have been my online friend for years and your advice, prayers, and encouragement during my husband's deployment were so valuable to me. Thank you for always listening to my rants via Facebook message, and thank you for being there to read so many of my blog posts; making sure they sounded good and adding your input from being a veteran army wife. Thank you for the chapters you contributed to this book, I know that so many lives will be touched by your words and by having them in this book. You are someone I will always look up to. Thank you.

Alane, thank you so much for your encouragement and help with this book. I am so glad God led me to work with you as my publishing coach. You have been so much fun to work with and I feel that I have known you for a lot longer than the few months we have chatted online! Thank you for your ministry and all that you have done to work with me and my book. Thank you for your patience.

Jonathan, thank you for your support and understanding during the writing of this book. Thank you for being you and for loving me unconditionally. I love you, forever and always.

To my blog readers: Thank you for all the encouragement you gave to me when writing these posts. The stories and heartbreaks you shared with me helped me grow and gave me a better understanding of military life. Thank you for reading, you all encourage me and bless me more than you will know.

Last, but not least, I am so thankful for God's help. Without Him, I would never have gotten through each weary day of deployment and without Him I would never have finished this book. So thankful for His unconditional love that never fails me.

Table of Contents

Preface

If you are reading this book, then you are most likely a military spouse whose family just received deployment orders or you are currently experiencing a deployment. Maybe this is your first deployment, or maybe you are a veteran military spouse who has done this many times and you know what to expect this time around. Either way, this book is for you.

This book is divided into three sections: pre-deployment, deployment, and post-deployment. Feel free to read from beginning to end or start from the section that corresponds with the stage of deployment you are currently in. As you read through this book, I suggest starting a deployment journal, one in which you can write your thoughts and prayers, and journal through this deployment.

Let this book be your guide to your journey through deployment. Let it help lift you up and encourage you along the way, and know you are not alone. Whatever stage of deployment you are in, know that you are in my prayers. I have been there and I know what it's like. Don't give up and stay strong in Christ. He will get you through.

Sincerely,

Kathryn

Pre-Deployment

Chapter 1:
ORDERS

Shock.

Anger.

Disappointment.

This is what was running through my mind when my husband, Jon, told me he received orders for his first deployment. It was a beautiful, sunny day in June and our families would arrive for my son's first birthday party the next day.

My husband came home for lunch, walked through the door, and told me he received deployment orders.

Just like that.

I am not sure what I expected, but even though it was expected he would go sometime that year, I was still surprised when he told me. For the previous three years, I had grown complacent and happy with our military life. That July marked three years since Jon joined the United States Air Force and, until that year, he had yet to deploy.

My feelings of disbelief and anger were normal that day, and so are yours. You will go through a rough time after hearing the news. It's not easy to hear that your spouse is going away and I'm sure it's not easy for them to tell you they are leaving. Keep in mind that they are hurting, too. Don't pull away, but use this time to grow closer together.

Cry if you must, be angry if you must, but know that you are NOT alone. Take a deep breath. You can do this. You will learn how to get through the roller coaster of feelings and emotions that come when you first get the news. You will learn how to accept and embrace it.

Chapter 2:
EMOTIONAL STAGES OF PRE-DEPLOYMENT

So you have the deployment orders. You even may have an official departure date. Now it's time to deal with and work through all the emotions you're feeling. You have to learn how to cope.

I've watched a lot friends go through deployment. I have seen different people deal with the news, deal with the pre-deployment stress, emotions, and anything else that comes along the way. Everyone deals with these situations differently and there are many emotional stages that military spouses go through before deployment.

If you have gone through a deployment before, these might sound familiar or maybe you might relate better to one of these 7 Stages of Emotional Deployment. Here are the emotional stages I went through upon receiving news of my husband's deployment. You may have experienced something similar if you have been through a deployment, or you might experience something completely different. We all handle deployment in different ways.

1. Denial

Your spouse comes home with orders and tells you they will be deploying. You think:

This is a joke.

They're just kidding, right?

There is no way they got orders...again.

Nope, there must have been a mistake.

Surely there was a mix-up.

These are really for someone else. I just know they are.

2. Disbelief

After your spouse assures you it's not a joke, you move on to the next stage. You think:

I can't believe this is happening.

How could this happen so soon?

Why did this happen to us?

I just can't believe it.

Maybe this is just a dream...

Pinch Nope, definitely not a dream.

3. Anger

Soon, your disbelief turns into anger. You are looking for someone to blame, so you blame the military and maybe even your spouse. You think:

I hate the military.

I hate this life.

Why did my spouse choose this?

Why are they leaving me?

They can't leave me like this.

I can't do this on my own.

We will never get this time back again.

I will never get past this.

4. Sadness

Then, your anger turns to sadness, and eventually, tears. You think:

I can't do this.

I don't want to do this.

I don't want to be alone.

What am I going to do?

What happens if something goes wrong?

What if there is an emergency?

I CANNOT do this!

5. Acceptance

But in the end, you slowly move into acceptance. You know it's happening whether you want it to or not. You think:

Okay, I can do this.

I don't want to do this, but I can do this.

We are going to make it through.

Let's get this deployment going.

The sooner they are gone, the sooner they can be back.

You get the countdowns ready, make all your plans, keep busy, and you do it. And you do it well. You are a military spouse and you can get through this!

You may be thinking, "This all sounds great, but how do I work through all of that?" The answer: with time and a lot of patience. Some days may seem better than others; sometimes you may think you have moved through a stage only to backtrack one or two. That's okay. Eventually, you will move to acceptance, and with that acceptance, comes peace.

Keep in mind your spouse will be working through his own emotions. He may not admit it, but he has to go through some emotional stages as well. He wants to make sure his family is going to be well cared for and that you are going to be emotionally strong enough for him to leave behind. Be there for each other. Work together through this roller coaster of emotions. You may find it draws you both closer together than you ever imagined!

The Reality of Deployment

As you get closer to your spouse's deployment, reality will set in. Your head may be telling you, I can't do this. But in your heart, I think you know that's not true. You can do this–even if it's hard. You will do this and you will do it well!

The reality of deployment hit me hard.

I wished...he could stay here and never leave again.

Reality was...that just couldn't happen. Every family has some kind of time apart even if sometimes it is short and sometimes it is long.

I wished...I had family that lived closer to help me get through.

Reality was...I didn't. Not everyone can live close to their family. I couldn't always depend on family; I had to learn to be independent.

I wished...that the deployment was shorter.

Reality was...it could have been longer, and I should have been thankful.

I wished...there was a better time for this to happen.

Reality was...there will never be a better time for a deployment.

I wished...I didn't have to do this.

Reality was...I didn't really have an option. I learned that I would get through it because I had to, and because God was with me.

God knew a long time ago that your deployment would come. Maybe the things that have happened in your life have prepared you to be stronger so that you could get through this with God's help.

A deployment is a big deal. Being a single parent for the next several months or longer is a big deal, but at the end of this, you are going to be a stronger person.

You are going to be able to say, "God is good no matter what." You are going to be able to look back at what you overcame and say, "Wow. I did that."

No military spouse wants to deal with deployment, but the reality is we have no choice in the matter. But maybe, just maybe, something good will come from this. God is in control and He knows what is going to happen.

The reality is it won't be easy. The reality is that it's going to be really hard. But there is also the reality that God is still here and walking alongside you. You are not alone.

Chapter 3:
PREPARING FOR DEPLOYMENT

By now your mind is probably reeling with everything you need and want to prepare before your husband deploys. I remember feeling the same way. After our first deployment, I realized what I could do differently to prepare for the next deployments that came along. Yes, I believe you can be prepared for deployment.

Being ready for deployment is like being ready to jump off a ten-story building: it's not going to happen. I don't think you can ever be ready for deployment, but I do believe you can be prepared. There are a lot of ways you can prepare for deployment.

1. Talk and discuss.

This is first on the list because I believe it is that important. As soon as your spouse gets deployment orders, have a conversation about how you both feel. If they are not open to discussing it, wait until they are ready and talk to a friend or family member about how you are feeling.

When talking to family or friends, don't forget about OPSEC! OPSEC, which stands for Operational Security, means to be careful about what you say and share with others about your spouse's mission, location, and any other troop movement.

When it's time, and you both are ready, make a list of everything you need to discuss about deployment and everything you will need to do while your spouse is gone.

Here are some suggested topics for you to talk about:

Feelings:

- How you both feel about deployment
- Ways you both can cope
- Ways you both can encourage and support each other throughout the deployment
- How to tell extended family members about the deployment orders (parents, grandparents, etc.)

Communication:

- What to do if there is limited communication once your spouse is deployed
- Ways your spouse would like to communicate with you
- How frequently you both would like to talk to each other

Emergency Situations:

- What to do if there is an emergency situation (for example, a miscarriage, death of a family member, hospitalization of a family member, etc.)

- What other family members should be contacted if there is an emergency
- What to do if the car breaks down, where to take it to get fixed, etc.

Finances:

- Who will be in charge of the finances
- What you should do if there is an emergency situation requiring a large amount of money
- How to pay the bills
- Items needing to be paid while your spouse is gone (a lease/rent, car tags renewed, insurances, etc.)
- Discuss if you are saving for something special such as a post-deployment vacation, Christmas presents for the kids, etc.
- Make a list of passwords for computers, credit cards, and bank websites, etc.

Children:

- How to tell the kids that their parent has orders
- How to handle and deal with discipline issues that may come up while your spouse is gone
- Ways to help your kids through deployment
- What to tell the kids throughout the deployment when they ask, "Where is Daddy/Mommy?" and "When will he/she be home?"
- How to explain OPSEC to your kids

Traveling:

- Where the family will stay/travel to when your spouse is gone and for how long
- Who will come and visit/stay while your spouse is gone and for how long

Homecoming:

- Who your spouse wants at the homecoming
- If your spouse wants a homecoming party or a more quiet reception

Our first deployment was full of surprises I was not prepared for. The first week after my husband left, our lease ran out, my car started smoking, my mom and brothers were in a car accident, and I got locked out of our main joint bank account! You can bet I had no idea how to handle all of that. Did I make it through? Of course. And now I know how to be prepared should any of it ever happen again.

All of that was just the beginning! Later in the deployment, my son was hospitalized, my husband's grandfather passed away, and my son had to be tested for autism. You never know what might happen while your spouse is deployed, so it's best to try to prepare for every situation so you will know what to do as each problem arises.

Another military wife, Jessica, suggests, "We try to talk a lot before he leaves about what we both expect as far as communication goes. Granted, we don't know what the situation will be like until he's there, but it's nice to have some idea of the expectations we both have as for when we/he can talk."

2. Make a plan.

I think the next best thing you can do before deployment is to make a plan. Plan out, as best as you can, the next months of your spouse's deployment. Decide if you are going to stay home or travel. Arrange travel plans as soon as possible so it's easier and less expensive. Begin looking for and interviewing sitters to give you breaks and to help you keep up with housework during the deployment. If it's a summer deployment, start planning fun summer activities and vacations. If it's during the school year, make sure you plan around school activities.

Don't forget to plan for holidays, anniversaries and birthdays. Do you want to be at home or with family? Do you want your family to come to you? Now is the time to start planning and talking about all of the options with your family members.

Plan your days. Do you want to have a job during this time? Join a club? Try something new? This is the time to plan all of that! There are classes you can take, get-togethers with friends you can plan, and much, much more. Start searching and planning now to fill up the calendar so that the days will go by faster during the deployment.

Jessica, a military wife, says, "I sign up for different classes and organizations to make sure I have plenty of activities to keep me busy while he's away."

3. Start saving and buying NOW.

This is one of those things I wished we knew about before our first deployment. The military gave my husband a huge list of things he needed to bring on deployment, from clothing items, uniforms and toiletries, to things like backpacks and bags to carry it all in. Unfortunately, the military does not pay for the list of stuff he must bring over – at least not in the Air Force. We were not prepared for the expense of what he needed just to get over there.

I also wish I had started looking around and saving for care package items before he left. Care packages are a lot more expensive than people let on and I was surprised at how much money I had to put into them. I'm not saying it's not worth it, because it definitely was, but it was a struggle to find cheap things to fill an entire box with and not break our budget!

My suggestion is to put money away as soon as you can for the things your husband is going to need. Start shopping the sales and look for items that would be good for care packages. The dollar store is a great place to start. Stock away the items you buy and watch as your pile grows!

Some care package ideas that we used are:

- Candies – make sure you buy kinds that won't melt
- Snacks – beef jerky, Pringles, crackers, and anything else that is individually wrapped and won't go bad
- Homemade cookies – make sure they are sealed nice and tight
- Toiletries – deodorant, small packs of tissues, and chap stick
- Holiday items
- Things to remind them of home
- Anything else your spouse might need or request!

4. Discuss things that need to get done before your spouse leaves.

Start making a list of things that need to be done before your spouse leaves on deployment to ensure that your household is in top running order.

Some items to discuss include:

- House maintenance
- Car maintenance: oil changes, tire pressure, etc.
- Renewing car tags before they expire
- Renewing your home lease if you have one
- Renewing Military IDs if necessary

Make an appointment with the legal office to create a Power of Attorney (POA) and will for both you and your spouse. Make sure you discuss what you want in each of your wills before you go to the legal office as it can be embarrassing to have to make and discuss last minute decisions while someone is sitting there with you.

Discuss hard things such as:

- What kind of POA you will choose
- Who will take care of your children in the event something happens to both you and your spouse
- How and where you and your spouse want to be buried

Catherine, a military spouse, suggests, "Make a list of 'honey-do' or maintenance items that need to be done around the house and to vehicles before the deployment. Update family pictures and pictures of

Daddy/Mommy and the kids. Try to set some time aside for a mini vacation or even a 'staycation' to make special memories before he/she leaves.

Don't forget to make sure computers, cell phones, and any other communication devices (Skype, camcorders, etc.) are in working order. Make sure a fully-stocked emergency kit is in the car along with updating the home tool kit for tackling basic things without having to hunt through all the tools.

Make a deployment binder that contains your spouse's deployment address, powers of attorney, updated wills, points of contact, itinerary, etc. At our other house, this also included a map of how to set out the sprinklers in the spring and summer for adequate lawn watering. At our new house, it included simplified directions on working the sprinkler system, when to change the air filters, etc.

We have a finance meeting to go over what funds he will need while there and when I will transfer them. I manage finances 100% of the time so there is no change of hands there, but he leaves his joint account card at home and takes one that is for a separate account. I transfer funds he needs to that card. This helps prevent us being affected in a huge way if his card is lost or stolen, because I can instantly transfer all funds back to the joint account.

We also update passports for all family members so that, if needed, we can travel out of the country. For a child to get a passport, both parents must be present or a form must be signed and notarized by the parent not present. You have to apply for the passport within 30 to 90 days of that form being filled out.

Don't forget to grab a couple of international phone cards (Sam's club has the best rates) for your spouse to use if needed during travel."

Preparing for Changes

One of the most important things to remember when preparing for deployment is that the military is always changing plans. They change dates, they change orders, and they may even change the place to which your spouse deploys. Some of these changes may be last-minute changes; some may be changed a few days after you first receive the news. Things may change five times between your pre-deployment stage and your spouse's actual departure date. All you can do is go with the flow.

When my husband was preparing for his first deployment, his deployment date changed to a later date only one week before he was supposed to leave. I was very upset. Preparing for these changes is important as it can be quite a shock if you are not used to it. If you understand that the military does change and will change, it will much easier for you to be flexible enough to keep up with it!

When you find out that your spouse is deploying, you have that date stuck in your head. You think about that date and it's constantly on your mind. You prepare yourself mentally and emotionally, and when that date gets closer, you do everything you can to make the most of the time you have left. But when that date changes, the mind games start and you get on that roller coaster of emotions.

I am one of those people who likes to be prepared. I have to know what is going on ahead of time; I have to have a plan. Military life is the total opposite of that and it has caused me to realize that I can't always be a planner. I won't always know what's going to happen because things change.

The goodbyes had been said, the bags had been packed, and last minute preparations were in place, but my husband's deployment date changed several times in a matter of two days. The date didn't change to an earlier time like I had almost thought to expect, but to a date over a week later. It wasn't that big of a change, I know, but to prepare yourself and spend all those last moments doing what you can to make them last, it's almost as though I didn't know what to do with the extra time.

I had a sitter scheduled and a friend at the ready so I didn't have to drive back from the airport alone–but it all changed. I was thankful for more time together, but all my plans had gone away.

Two verses came to mind in this situation:

> *"For my thoughts are not your thoughts, nor are your ways my ways, says the Lord. For as the heavens are higher than the earth, so are my ways higher than your ways, and my thoughts than your thoughts."*
> – Isaiah 55:8,9 (NKJV)

> *"For I know the thoughts that I think toward you, says the Lord, thoughts of peace and not of evil to give you a future and a hope."*
> – Jeremiah 29:11 (NKJV)

God knows what's going on and He knows how I felt and how you feel. He is there even when the date changes and your emotions are going up and down.

Don't Let the Stress Get You Down!

It's very easy to get overwhelmed and stressed when going through the pre-deployment stage. Sometimes it can be a struggle not to be discouraged.

How can you handle pre-deployment stress?

1. Pray.

I will be honest: there were times I just didn't feel like praying. I felt stressed, overwhelmed and certainly not in the mood to pray. But why wait? Isn't that a good time to bring it all to God? I think so!

2. Don't let it build up.

This is one I am still learning. Letting your feelings and emotions build up inside of you just makes things worse. Soon enough, all those thoughts and feelings are going to have to come out – and it's probably not going to be pretty. Before those feelings build up, talk to someone about them!

3. Talk to someone.

I know that in the military community, you are not supposed to put a lot on your spouse before or during a deployment. They have to focus on the mission. However, I believe that is not always right. Keeping everything in is not good, and talking things over with your spouse is a good stress reliever for both of you. You can also talk to a pastor or counselor if you are having trouble handling things. Sometimes just having someone to vent to, bounce ideas off of, or pray for you is just what you need to feel better.

Chapter 4:
PREPARING FOR THE WORST CASE SCENARIO

No matter how prepared you try to be, sometimes there will still be emergencies. Knowing how to react during these times is important and being ready for them will make you feel better, too. My friend, Aprille, has some great tips on preparing for the worst case scenario which she shares in this chapter.

One way you can prepare for deployment is by compiling an "In Case of Emergency" form.

I did not do this until my husband deployed to Afghanistan the second time leaving me at home with a four-month-old baby. While I definitely feared for my husband's safety, the most disturbing image that kept being replayed in my overactive imagination was of my son awake and crying, but unharmed, in the backseat of my car at the scene of an accident while I laid in the front unconscious and in need of medical attention.

It absolutely terrified me! Fortunately, I attended an *Operation Faithful Support* session which discussed how to deal with fears during deployment. One of the suggestions was to do what you can to minimize those fears. I went home that evening and sat down on my computer to type out an ICE, or In Case of Emergency, form. From then on, my fears were allayed.

Sometimes, the answer to a "What if?" question is to simply be more realistic in the asking. What if the car accident actually happens? What if I have to be rushed to the hospital for surgery? What if I am in a coma? What would the police and doctors do? Would they just default and send my child to social services? Who would they look for? What information would they need in order to make sure that my child and I are cared for and safe? And what can I do to make it easy on them so they don't have to go scrambling for information?

I promise if you do something like this, it will greatly put your mind at ease. This is not exclusively for military families. I believe every family should have a form like this that is updated once or twice a year and kept on-hand (in addition to insurance forms, wills, and POAs) in case of an emergency.

What to include:

- The names, birthdates, social security numbers, blood types, food or medical allergies, and any preexisting medical conditions for all of your immediate family members

- Your home address, phone numbers, and cell phone numbers

- Your next-of-kin (I included both my husband's parents and my parents), their addresses and phone numbers (home and cell phone)

- Your medical insurance information

- Name and contact information of your primary care physicians and your local hospital or post-clinic

- Business or unit information including staff duty phone numbers, rear detachment contact numbers, unit designations, and, if your husband is deployed, rear detachment and Red Cross emergency contact information

- A detailed plan-of-action for what you would like emergency personnel to do in case of your absence

For example, mine read this way:

In the event that we (our names) are incapacitated, please follow the following steps:

- Arrange for immediate and short-term childcare by calling [insert name and contact information for a local emergency contact]. If you cannot reach her, please call [insert name and contact information for another local emergency contact]. I also put the information for the local on-post Army child care.

- Notify next-of-kin. Once they arrive, please place [children] in their direct care. List which next-of-kin you would prefer to care for your children in the event of an emergency.

- Notify my landlords [list their names and phone numbers] to get access to the house.

- Notify husband's chain of command (or other place of employment).

Also add personal information about your family and especially your children, for anyone who may end up caring for them:

Feeding:

- Infants: Include how often and how much they should be fed. Formula: How much? How often? What brand? Breastfeeding: Is there stored milk anywhere? If so, how often and how much should they be fed? Older babies: What solid foods can they eat? What do they prefer? Any juice?

- Children: List food likes and dislikes and food allergies

- Scheduling and sleeping: When do they nap? What is a normal bedtime?

- Locations of important items in your home (diapers, wipes, toys, and medicines)

- Any medications your children are taking including dosages

Print several copies of this form and place in key places in your house and car. I actually keep two forms in the car, one in the glove compartment and one in the trunk (You know, in case half of the car gets engulfed in flames, of course!). I have one hanging on the refrigerator and one in the hallway closet.

This may seem slightly obsessive, and it may be. But at the very least, it might help allay some of your fears, especially if you are going through a deployment. Above all, our trust needs to be in God. He is greater and more powerful than any emergency forms, and I know that He will take care of my family and your family.

Chapter 5:
PREPARING YOUR KIDS FOR DEPLOYMENT

When a dear friend of mine welcomed home her deployed husband for an R&R, it made me start to think. Her son was only a couple of months younger than mine, and I started thinking about all the things her husband had missed so far in their son's life while he was gone. Birthdays, milestones, first words... a lot can happen in eight months!

It made me start thinking about my son, Adam, and how he would deal with his father being away on his first deployment. At the time, Adam was only 14 months old. Since he is such a Daddy's boy, I was worried about how he would deal with him being away for so long.

I wished I could protect him. I wished I could stop it from happening to him. As an adult, I can deal with a deployment in my own way, but how was he supposed to deal, being just a little boy? Even though he knew Daddy was gone, he didn't fully understand. And even though he saw Daddy occasionally on Skype and heard his voice on the phone a few times, I wasn't sure how to get him to understand that his dad would be back, that he had not left for good, and that he still loved him very much even though he was far away.

I love my son so much. I didn't want to see him go through the rigors of deployment. I wanted to shield him as much as I could, but it felt impossible. I knew there would be other deployments, other times apart. This is what military life is all about. It's about learning to adapt, learning to press on, and learning that my responsibility is being the best parent I can be while my spouse is away.

As I thought again about my friend's son being reunited with his dad, and as I looked through their homecoming pictures, I saw how happy the little boy was. He didn't care that his dad had been gone; he was just happy that he had returned. He wasn't thinking of all the missed moments; he was looking forward to holding his dad's hand and playing with him again.

I grew a little more confident that it would be the same for my son. My hope was and still is that he will not grow up thinking about all the times Daddy was away, but that he will remember all the good times they spent together: the playing, wrestling, laughing, tickling, and everything in between! Those are the moments that create memories. Those are the things my son loves about his dad.

It's also important for the military parent to feel close to the child. Even at a young age, while your children may not remember the deployment or understand what's happening, the military parent does and he still needs that connection. I know my husband was so worried about our son not remembering who he was when he got home. I think because of both of our efforts, Adam had an easier transition once Daddy did come home. Adam seemed so happy to see him again.

There are a lot of things you can do to help your kids get through deployments. As the child grows older and goes through more deployments, you may have to change the way you handle it.

Seven Ways to Help
Your Child Through Deployment

1. Use photos.

Keep a "Photo a Day While Daddy/Mommy Is Away" album either on Facebook or on a private page where you can post a photo of your child every day for your spouse to see. Try to capture one memory per day, either of what you did that day or just of your child being cute. My husband loved being able to see the photos of my son doing new or cute things. The hard thing is remembering to take a picture every day. I was really good about it in the beginning, but then I forgot a lot during the second half of the deployment.

Hang up photos of your spouse in your child's room or around the house where your child can see them. A friend of mine had a huge poster of her husband that she hung in her son's room during deployment. It was right at his level so he could give Daddy "kisses" every day. You can also make a small non-breakable album filled with pictures of Daddy/Mommy or of your child and Daddy/Mommy together so that your child can look at it. I know my son loves looking at photos of us and is always dragging our albums around the house!

Also, use your camera or your phone's camera to capture little videos throughout the day. I would post videos of new things my son was doing on Facebook and my husband could log on and watch them whenever he had time. He loved seeing those little bits of home and it made him feel closer to us.

2. Talk about your spouse all the time!

Once my husband left, I made sure I talked about him every day to my son. Even though Adam probably didn't understand everything I was saying, I would tell him Daddy loved him, Daddy was thinking about him, Daddy was working hard for us, and Daddy was going to call soon. I just talked him up as much as I could.

3. Let your child help with care packages.

Ask your child what he or she would like to send to their Daddy/Mommy. Take them to the dollar store to pick out things to put in the care packages. My son was too little for any of the above, but I did let him color pictures for Daddy. Then, I would sign his name and write, "I love you, Daddy!" and send it off with each care package. My husband loved it!

4. Skype.

As a military family, you probably know how valuable Skype or any other video program can be. We used Skype so that my husband could talk to and watch Adam play. My son couldn't talk at the time, but he was able to see Daddy almost every day. My husband was able to watch Adam play as I followed him around the house with my laptop.

5. Daddy Dolls.

Daddy Dolls are a life-saver during deployment! You submit a picture of your military member in uniform and *Daddy Dolls, Inc.* will put the picture on a stuffed and huggable doll. My son loves his Daddy Doll and still carries it all around the house. He slept with it every night during the first deployment and gave it hugs and kisses. It's a great way to help your child get through deployment!

6. Pre-recorded Books.

A family member gave us a book called Together at Heart by Editors of Publications International Ltd. before my husband deployed. Together at Heart features Elmo from Sesame Street. His dad leaves on a trip and the book goes through all the ways that Elmo and his dad stayed close together at heart even though they were far apart. It is a very sweet book and perfect for deployment!

It was a book that you could record yourself reading. We had never used one before and were excited to see how it worked. My husband recorded himself reading the book and, after he deployed, my son listened to it every day. It is still his favorite book.

7. Have another male or female role model around your child.

It's beneficial to have another male or female role model for your child while your spouse is away, depending on if it's their mom or dad who is deployed. It's not to replace Daddy/Mommy, but to have that other adult influence that children need.

When my husband was deployed, I had a few older boys who would come over and play with Adam and he loved that rough -and-tumble time. Ask around at your church or ask your friends if any of them would be able to pick up that role while your spouse is deployed.

More ideas from fellow military moms:

"When I had young kids during deployment, we took them to Build-a-Bear and had my hubby record a message to them inside a bear we dressed in camo. They took it everywhere and listened to it every night during deployments and all separations. There was no Skype or video program at the time, so it was often the only chance they had to hear his voice while he was gone. We also made sure to have one or two close male friends who committed to regularly spend time with the kids, especially the boys – not as a replacement, but as a male role model during his absence." – *Jane*

"We bought Daddy Dolls and that seemed to help. We also used Skype. Jake loved to sit on the computer desk and kiss the screen when talking to his dad. We did a recorded Hallmark book, too, and they loved it. It is so used that the binding is broken." – *Miranda*

"I bought a fabric photo album for each child filled with photos of them with their dad. They were carried everywhere! We also had Daddy Dolls and recorded books. I have a Zoodles account on my phone. Daddy read stories and they were able to see and hear him reading, as well as the story book." – *Angie*

"When my kids were young, my husband recorded videos of himself reading and talking to them. We watched the videos every night and it really helped them. We also had Daddy Dolls that they still sleep with to this day. I also made both kids a bulletin board of pictures of just them with Daddy. They loved looking at it. I encouraged them to "write" letters to Daddy and draw him pictures. Once a month, I took them to the dollar store and let them pick out items just from them to send to Daddy. That was the most fun! They enjoyed being a part of sending stuff to Daddy and decorating the box." – *Jessica*

"I have three children under the age of three years old. I did not expect them to miss my husband much because of their ages, but they did! I wish I had prepared myself more to expect it. My husband takes a picture of himself holding whatever we send – art work or the Build-a-Bear, and we print it out and I give them each their own picture. It goes everywhere with them just like a favorite toy. He also recorded himself playing peek-a-boo in the house and they love that video." – *Trish*

Deployment

Chapter 6:
SAYING GOODBYE

Your spouse's dreaded departure date has finally arrived and it's time to say goodbye. Every family has a different way of dealing with it and a different way of saying goodbye. Some families may go to the airport or the base, while some may say goodbye at home. Everybody is different and there is no wrong way to do it. Just make sure that your last words together are peaceful ones.

For my husband's first deployment, I choose to leave my 16-month-old home with a sitter and make the two-hour drive to the airport with him. My husband was able to have a special goodbye at home with my son and one later on with me at the airport. Now that my son is a lot older, we may do things differently the next time around, but for the first deployment, it worked well.

This is my story of that day – the day we said goodbye for seven months. My hope is that in sharing it with you, you will not feel alone and that you may even feel encouraged.

My Goodbye Story

I did not realize that saying goodbye, or "See you later..." as it is known in military circles, would be so hard. Sure, no goodbye is ever easy, but this – this was a lot harder than I ever anticipated. And you know what the ironic thing is? Saying goodbye wasn't even the hardest part.

I had a ton to do that morning. I woke up, put myself in super-wife mode and did what I had to do. I even made it through my shower without crying. I just felt numb. I had a list of things to do that morning on top of getting ready. I had to run to the store to get my son more baby food and milk, pick up water-proof mascara (because apparently I didn't have any), pick up my friend who was coming with us so I didn't have to drive home alone from the airport, and pick up my son's babysitter.

I ran my errands and picked up my friend, who was probably wondering why I wasn't crying yet. I was in my zone; I was not going to cry until it was absolutely necessary. We got home, I ran over the schedule with my son's sitter, and tried to think of anything else that could prevent us from leaving any sooner than we had to. My friend knew what I was doing. So did my husband, and he made us leave.

The two-hour drive to the airport wasn't bad. It was filled with chatter about the day and about life. We stopped for breakfast on the way to the airport, and that was when I had a few moments to think. Bad idea. My stomach was tied in knots, and for a moment I didn't even want to eat. But I did. We were back on the road quicker than I hoped for and we soon arrived at the airport.

As we were getting out of the car, my stomach felt sick. I was wishing I hadn't eaten. It was a quick walk into the airport where my husband dropped off his bags. There were no lines and everything was going by too fast. I wanted to beg him to slow down and to take his time, to do anything that could give us just a few more minutes together.

We slowly made our way toward security. My friend took several pictures. I wasn't sure whether to laugh or cry. I wanted to look back and remember this, remember how God got me through, and remember how strong I was.

My husband and I walked closer to the security entrance alone, and then the time had come. I knew: this was it. And the tears came. Nothing up until that point had mattered because at that last moment you realize everything you have is going away. I had held it together up until then and I just told him how badly I didn't want him to go. My husband tried to make me laugh, tried to make me feel better, but I know it was hard for him, too. I clung to him, hugging him not once, not twice, not even three times, but more like six or seven times. I could not let him go. Letting go and watching him walk away: that was the hardest part.

Eventually, I did let go, and once I did I knew there was no turning back. I was still wiping tears by the time I made it back to my friend. She gave me a hug and told me everything was going to be okay. The hardest part was over now, and I slowly slipped back into super-wife mode.

The rest of the day went by without incident. We made it home, and I asked my friend if she would come stay at my house for a bit. I didn't want to be alone. We chatted and made pumpkin bread. I felt like I was a robot just going through the motions. I was in a fog, but so eager to keep busy so I didn't have to think.

That night after I put my son to bed, I went to my room, laid down on my bed and cried. I was finally able to let go, at least a little. I had been strong for myself, my husband, and my son, and now it was time to let go. I gave myself a few more minutes in bed, and then decided I needed to press on. I got up, ate some dinner, and went on into the fog that I called life at the moment.

My Goodbye to My Love

I read somewhere that "goodbye" is the shortened form of "God be with you." Honey, I know God was with you, and I know God is with you now. I know that He will protect you, and get you through this even better than I could ever imagine. It's not my job to be "God" and I'm sure glad it's not. He is going to take care of you even better than I could ever do. Just remember my touch, remember my kiss, and always know that I love you.

Chapter 7:
ENCOURAGEMENT FOR DEPLOYMENT

The first few weeks after my husband left were the hardest. The first few days, I had friends, appointments, and errands that kept me busy, but then there wasn't much to do. I realized this was only the first week and I planned on getting into a good schedule soon. My husband had arrived safe and sound, and I knew he was getting settled into his new schedule as well.

But with the quiet house and the instant loneliness, some of the biggest fears and questions I had were this: How can I keep my marriage strong when my spouse and I have such little contact? What if we grow apart? What if we change?

I knew I was not the only one who had thought this way, so I asked the question on one of my online Christian military support groups.

I asked, "I am really discouraged because my husband and I have not been able to talk for any longer than two minutes at a time. I am assuming that maybe it's like this for everyone's deployment, but I don't see how you can keep a marriage alive when this is all there is to put into it. So I guess my question is this: How do you keep your marriage going when you can't even talk? Sure, I can write e-mails and letters, and send pictures, but marriage is two-sided and I can't help but ask myself, what is it going to be like by the end of this deployment? What do you all do?"

I received some supportive responses, and I hope they encourage you, too.

From Sara Horn:

"First, remember you are still in the first week. That first week is ALWAYS hard. Sometimes the first month is. He's adjusting to where he is and you're adjusting to the fact that he's not with you. Also, deployment is definitely a give and take, and often, you do feel like you're giving a whole lot. But give it time. He's going to get his footing, and both of you will figure out the rhythm of what communication is going to be like while he's gone. It depends on where he is and what they have available.

The biggest lesson I've learned from the two deployments I've been through is that you CAN'T take it personally. You just can't. You'll tear yourself up, and you'll add more stress to your husband's situation. Deployments are just seasons. As hard as it feels right now, it will eventually end, and your sweet hubby will be back in your arms (and the homecoming is a wonderful thing – you can't beat that rush when you see him back in front of you!). And yes, the letters and the e-mails are good. I think I heard recently of one wife who wrote an e-mail every day just letting her husband know how the day went. This is a good thing to do – it keeps you in touch with your husband, and lets him know you're thinking about him.

The last thing I'll say is something I had to learn the hard way in our first deployment. Deployments are a great lesson in showing us where we place God, and where we place our husbands. What I mean is, during my first experience with deployment, my husband was my absolute world, and when I couldn't hear from him, or didn't feel like he was there supporting me, it crushed me! But God taught me slowly, but surely, that my priorities were out of whack – my trust, my focus, my hope, needed to be on God and my support needed to go to my husband. Now, that didn't mean I still didn't expect my husband to try or that he was off the hook for 10 months – no way! But it meant that I stopped putting all my hope in my husband, and instead, I put it in God. And things got a LOT better.

Deployment can be extremely frustrating and heartbreaking. We have to remember where our source of joy really comes from – God. And He's with us no matter what."

My Response:

"I guess I am just scared our marriage is not going to be what it used to be by the time this deployment is done. I understand he might not have a lot of time, and I totally understand I will be putting more into it right now, but what if we hardly know each other by the end? I just know between his shifts, his online classes, and who knows what else, we may barely ever get to talk."

From Sara Horn:

"These are totally normal feelings. And I think a lot of us struggle with those thoughts. But you have to focus on the closeness you had as a couple before he left and trust that you'll have that when he gets back, because you're going to do the things you need to do to keep that communication going in between. What I find is that the couples who were close before usually are still close afterwards. It's the couples who are struggling before that often go one of two ways – either deployment makes them realize the importance of what they have and they get closer, or it drives them further apart. You're going to be absolutely fine. Focus on what God wants to teach you during this time apart and how you can still show love and support to him. It's going to be a growing time, but you're going to step back at the end of all of it, and just say, 'Wow, God is good.'"

From Aprille:

"You have to remember, too, that your marriage is a living organism. Your marriage will NOT be what it was before – and you have to kind of get some of those expectations out of your head. It can be affected by deployment in both positive and negative ways. It will be different. Does that mean it's bad? No. There will be good things, bad things, and even new things you will have to adjust to when he comes home. And your marriage will be different. But it can be better."

From Tia:

"I am so sorry you are struggling with this. We have all been there at some point. I am struggling with the change in relationship, too, and this is my third deployment. Until yesterday, I had a picture of me and my husband kissing on our honeymoon as my profile picture, because I wanted to feel that exact way again, but we have changed in the past seven years. People change, and deployments are just another way that happens. But it does happen to all marriages. He changes, then everyone adjusts; you change, then everyone adjusts. Then you both change. Sometimes your dedication to God and your marriage will be the only thing that is constant. That is not to say that your marriage will change THIS year. It might not, but if it does, it will be okay."

From Kelly:

"I understand what you're going through. I've realized that there has to be different expectations during deployment. Be confident in the love and relationship that you and your husband have when he IS home. Things are different just for right now. Pray, pray, pray that God will protect your marriage and keep the two of you close in each other's hearts. God is also your strength to help you deal with things on your own when your husband is gone. As a spouse and parent, He wants us to bring our concerns to Him first, and try to figure things out with Him first. God loves you and will get you through this."

From Rebecca:

"I can understand your fear about what your marriage is going to be like after a long period of separation and little communication. I realized I could be 'doing' all the right things to make a good marriage, but I had to place my faith in God to protect and grow my marriage. It feels really foolish, and I really wanted to 'do' something. I was challenged that God, who was able to save me and do an amazing work in redeeming me to His image, is the same God who will do His work in preserving our marriage.

Sure, as a military spouse I am responsible to keep writing letters, sending packages, writing e-mails, sending pictures, and being as creative as humanly possible to encourage and love my husband halfway across the world. But ultimately, I can't place my confidence in those things. I can't do enough of those things to make my marriage good or keep it good. I have to place my faith in God to continue to grow our marriage, and really I wouldn't want the responsibility to all fall on what I do or even what my husband did because I know we would fail each other.

I don't mean to sound all 'spiritual' on you. I am right there with you; the fear and pain of your heart being ripped apart and the fear that this marriage that means so much to you, that you have worked so hard for, and probably abandoned families and friends for, will be so different when he gets back. God knows all of that!

I'll be praying for you that you will be able to talk with your husband but I'll also be praying that you will be able to place your faith in God to preserve and grow your marriage."

From Andrea:

"I'm just another military wife, but felt compelled to share a message with you and anyone else who might need to hear this. When my husband deployed last year, I felt so alone. And even though it was his second deployment, I was still unable to mentally and emotionally prepare myself completely. I got this e-mail about a month after he left and I have kept it this entire time because there were some days I would have to go back and read it again...and again...and again:

'Both times my husband left, I gave myself permission to cry. After I had a big cry, I'd think to myself, Okay, that's enough! I'm pulling myself together and getting through this day. I can't say that pep talk worked the entire day each time, but it did help! Tears form in my eyes just thinking about what you're going through. I've been there, but not with kids. I can't imagine how you feel today. I'm praying for you that God will hold you up and keep you strong over the next year. Some of my closest moments to God have been in times when my husband was gone. I pray that you are blessed with moments like that.

I also want to share a bit of wisdom my dad shared with me the last time my husband was gone. He told me that people would be watching how I handle the situation. Will it glorify God or will I crumble and not trust Him? I can't say that every moment he was gone glorified God. I'm human. But it did give me motivation to allow God to use me in that time. It gave me the strength to show people who God is through my struggles. I know that's a lot to think about and not AT ALL what you want to do today. Today, cry, be mad, and be scared because I know that's what you must truly be feeling.'"

I received a lot of other messages and answers and notes of encouragement, but these are the ones that really stand out in my mind. I hope they can be an encouragement to you as well.

In One Word: Deployment

If this is your first time going through a deployment, you are going to learn so many things during this time. You will learn things about yourself, your spouse, and your family and friends. You will learn how to handle things that are thrown at you, and how to handle them without falling apart at the seams. You will learn that marriage takes work, it takes prayer, and it takes love and patience. If you are a mother, you will learn that being a mother is not as easy as maybe you once thought – especially while trying to parent alone. You will learn a lot.

In just the first four weeks that my husband was deployed, I did things I was never prepared to do. I never thought I would have to prepare myself to tell my husband that a family member of his had only six months to live. Sure, nothing prepares you for that, but finding the time between my husband's 12- to 18-hour work shifts, bad Skype connections, and several e-mails was hard.

I was not prepared to encourage my husband during times when I felt so discouraged that I had nothing to say. I was not prepared to fix cars, brake lights, internet connections, and video game consoles, but there I was troubleshooting with friends, family, and neighbors trying to figure out what had gone wrong. I was not even prepared for the changes my husband had been through where he was. Three different rooms, and approximately 15 different roommates later, I about had it and I'm sure he had, too. It was a complete mess. There was also his shift change, his sleeping patterns, and his job change.

Through all this, I realized it's all out of my control. None of this can be controlled by me. Not the things that happened, not the outcomes, and certainly not the future. I tried to control it, but I just couldn't and you can't either. I had to take a step back and say, "God, it's Yours."

And do you know what He said? "That's what I have been waiting for all along."

Chapter 8:
WHEN MURPHY STRIKES!

The Murphy's Law of deployment is what every military wife knows will happen as soon as her husband is gone. The car breaks down, the kids get sick, the dishwasher breaks, the dog throws up. Whatever it may be, it happens while he is gone.

Only one week after my husband left, the Murphy's Law of deployment began. It all started when I saw a post on Facebook from a woman on our base. She wrote about receiving a notice on her door about her house lease expiring. As soon as I saw it, I knew I had one on my door as well. I just knew it.

I had no idea the lease to our house on base could expire; I just figured we would live here until we got orders for a permanent change of station (PCS). Apparently, that's not how it works. Our lease had actually expired six months prior, but they were just then letting us know. Luckily, I was able to go to the housing office the next day to talk it over with them. All I needed to do was get a house inspection and sign a new lease with my POA.

It wasn't hard, but it almost gave me a heart attack to think about losing our home. Only a day or two later, I arrived at a friend's house to drop Adam off on my way to a yoga class on the base. My phone rang, and it was my brother at college telling me my mom and my other brother had been in a car accident. I almost dropped the phone. My mom and brother were okay, but the car was really damaged and my mom was issued a ticket.

The very next day, I was on my way to meet another friend for a play date and I stopped at the gas station on base right around the corner. Just as I was about to pump my gas, someone came up to me and told me my engine was smoking. My heart sunk. Up to this point I had refused to believe that any of this was the Murphy's Law of deployment, but now it was pretty much true. I had no clue about cars and had no idea what to do. A couple of guys tried to get my hood open, but none of us could figure it out. I decided to drive to the park to meet my friend like planned and see if anything else would happen with the car.

At the park, my friend suggested looking at the car manual to get the hood open. We both looked under the hood, but couldn't see anything wrong. Later that day, I went to pick up my friend from the base gate, and the car was making a bad hissing noise and had a burnt smell. After that, I decided it wasn't a good idea to drive the car anymore.

After getting the car towed, having to borrow a friend's car for a full week so I could continue taking my son to therapy, and all the other situations that came up later, I realized that this Murphy's Law thing was hard!

Only a few days later, Murphy struck again! I felt that to go through all this, God certainly must have had some crazy plans for me during deployment.

That night, my son threw up. It was his first time, so it was my first time ever dealing with it. Thank God for friends who let me call them at 11:30 at night to ask how to handle it and how to clean it up! I washed his blankie and then put him back to bed.

His stomach must have still been upset because I could hear him moving around. I was waiting for his blanket to dry, so I thought I would bring him down to wait until it was done. We sat on the stairs, and I thought I would turn on my computer to let him watch Veggie Tales for a few minutes. Bad idea. Without any warning at all, Adam threw up all over me, my computer, and the stairs.

I stood there for about five seconds in shock not sure of what to do. I quickly cleaned up Adam and myself, and tried to clean the computer while talking to my friend on the phone. I checked on Adam's blanket, gave him some Tylenol, and put him back to bed. He fell right back to sleep. I cleaned my computer the best I could – even taking a toothpick and cleaning between the keys – but it was pretty much done for. The keyboard wouldn't work.

By this time, I was freaking out. I wanted my computer to work because it was my only way to keep in touch with my husband except for my iPhone. I did everything I could for the computer, but since it was 1 a.m., I decided to go to bed. The next morning, I immediately called the clinic to make an appointment for Adam. At the same time, I was trying to find someone to fix my computer and realized that I was desperately in need of groceries.

Thankfully, a friend let me borrow her laptop until mine could get fixed. The doctors were able to help my son feel better and everything was calm for a little bit. During that time, all my friends on Facebook knew what had been going on since my husband deployed and one of my friends tagged me in a post called *A Military Wife's Promise*.

It was perfect for what I had been through and it described exactly what had been on my heart. If you are a military wife, I think you will understand. Megan Williams, the girl who wrote this, perfectly captured the feelings and emotions. I hope it helps you like it did me.

A Military Wife's Promise

"I cannot promise that I will not become frustrated when you leave me and the world seems to fall apart around me. I cannot promise that I will not curse those who sent you when the dryer breaks, and the transmission needs to be replaced, and the dog eats the couch all in the same week – most likely the week after you deploy. I cannot promise that the sand and mud that caked my floor will not cause me to give you harsh and rude thoughts. I cannot promise that my heart will not be torn in 1,200 different ways when you march away from me. I cannot promise that I will not let my anger show when you refuse to answer questions. I cannot promise that there won't be times when my heartache makes its presence known before my pride can mask it. I cannot promise that I will not show my worry and my concern when it is best for you not to see it. I cannot promise to understand why you do so many of the things you do.

But I can promise that for as many tears of sadness and frustration and anger that are shed, there will be double that of tears of pride. I can promise you that for every time you are away from me, I will learn to cherish the times that you are with me. In everything I will honor you and honor your sacrifice. I can promise to teach our children to do the same. I will use every moment that you are not with them to show them the amazing man that you are through my actions and my pride. I can promise that there will never be a night where you are not the subject of my final prayer and the keeper of my dreams. I promise to try to be understanding that there are many things I will never understand. I promise to keep you with me in everything and to do my best to keep grace in this life. I will be strong for you as you are strong for me and I will carry you with me in every moment until your sandy boots again sit just inside our door."

God taught me many lessons during this time. Deployment is hard, being independent is hard, but good friends and God's blessings got me through. Unfortunately, those were not the only things that happened while my husband was gone, but I am thankful that I can at least say I got through them with the help of good friends and God.

Chapter 9:
COPING WITH DEPLOYMENT

During my husband's deployment, I had so many people telling me things like, "You seem so calm," "You are so strong!" or, "I could never do that!" After going through so many different situations, and having my son sick and in the hospital, I thought to myself, Are you kidding me? If only you knew!

First of all, I am not calm. I am usually quite the opposite, although I am learning to keep it inside and not let my stress tumble out of me onto everything else. Second, I had no choice but to remain calm. I didn't think I could handle deployment, but I did, and I know that you can get through it just like I did! You know why? Because you don't have a choice either.

Each day before my husband left, I heard in the back of my head, *I can't do this, I can't do this, I can't do this*. I am no different from anyone else. I didn't think I could do it either, but I did one step at a time, and one day at a time, until it was finally over.

Ten Ways to Cope During Deployment

1. See a counselor.

I have been going to counseling since my husband first deployed, and I love it! Being able to talk things over and talk about people (yes, I said people) and things that bother me is so helpful. I didn't have my husband to talk to during the week, so it was nice to be able to get things off my chest, have someone talk to me and learn to cope with past and present situations.

My counselor always points me back to God, and sometimes I need that more than anything else. If you are interested in trying counseling, please know that it is covered by Tricare. It's not just for people with problems; it's for anyone who needs someone to talk to or even just help coping and getting by.

My encouragement to you is this: if you think you need counseling or you think you want counseling because you think it could benefit your life, then go! Don't let fear hold you back. Whether you are going to talk about something that has happened in your past, or because you have fear and anxiety, or to help you cope during a deployment, it is all important! I didn't just talk about my husband's deployment; I talked about other things as well: God, marriage, family, fears, excitement, and more. Talking these things over with someone and coming to understand things in my past has been a real blessing to my life and to my marriage.

2. Have a military wife as a mentor who is a sounding board for you.

During my husband's deployment, I had a friend and mentor who had been a military wife for over 20 years. She gave me advice and was there for me day or night. This poor woman heard from me at least once a day and sometimes as many as five times a day. She got phone calls from me in the middle of the night when I didn't know what to do, and she was so patient with me!

There were times when I just needed someone to talk to and she was always there to listen or give advice. If you can, find a mentor like that who has been through several years of military life. They will be a good person to go to when you have questions or just need someone to talk to who understands.

3. Pray… and pray and pray and pray.

If I had a dime for every time I prayed, "Lord, give me strength!" during our deployment, I would be rich! But seriously, prayer is what gets me through. Without my faith in God, knowing that He is listening and that He is there helping me, I would be lost. When you pray, it doesn't have to be this great, long prayer. Just tell Him how you feel. You will be amazed at the peace it brings to your heart when you place God first in your life and give everything over to Him.

4. Breathe.

I have an anxiety disorder. There are times when I know that I have been pushed to my limit – especially during deployment! Sometimes I just have to stand there and practice the breathing techniques I have learned so that I calm down.

It's called "candle breathing." You take a big, deep breath through your nose, hold it for a couple of seconds, and then blow it out through your mouth like you are blowing out a candle. After you do that a few times it helps put things in perspective. I do it when I feel like I am about to panic, or when things are getting too overwhelming for me. I also do it a lot when I am going to bed because it helps me relax so I can go to sleep. Try it sometime; you might be surprised how quickly it will help calm you down!

5. Exercise.

I have found that the times when I am upset or about to lose it, the best thing for me to do is to get on my treadmill and put all my energy into working out. I get off the treadmill feeling much better than when I started. It's a good use for all that negative energy and it feels good!

The times when I am stressed out the most have been some of my best work-outs because I really put everything I had into them. You don't have to do a crazy work-out to feel better; you can also go for a walk or find a local yoga class to attend.

6. Get out of the house.

Do you ever have that feeling where you just need to get out and do something? It happened a lot to me during deployment – especially when I was cooped up a lot with my son who was sick.

When I could, I would get out of the house and hang out with friends. No matter what it was, I got out and had a change of scenery. Sometimes being in the house for long periods of time can get to you. You need to get out, get fresh air, and see some people, places, and things. This helps to keep things in perspective, keep you busy, and keep the time flying by.

7. Try not to cry.

I'm not saying crying is bad, because sometimes you do need to let it all out. But for me, sometimes it doesn't stop and then I am sitting there crying and feeling sorry for myself all day.

When my husband's grandfather passed away, I had a moment where I started crying and could not stop. I was trying to wash the dishes while my son was sleeping and finally I just had to stop and sit on the floor because I was crying so hard. I find if I just push it out of my mind, and put that energy into something else, then I end up feeling better.

Of course, there are times when I do cry, and that's okay. But for the most part, I just put that into something else and it all comes out just fine. Also, talking to someone when you want to cry or while crying helps. It may sound silly, but that person is going to be understanding and want to help you through.

8. Talk to other military spouses who can understand what you're going through.

I have two friends who I know I can message anytime and they will listen and put things into perspective for me. Just knowing that they have been through and felt the same things as me is a huge encouragement. Find a friend who won't judge you, and who truly understands the military life, and talk to them whenever you are feeling low.

9. Find something to immerse yourself in.

For me, it was organizing, cleaning, decorating my house, and exercising. I put myself into cleaning and organizing my home because it needed it very badly and I wanted to learn to keep a nice home. Also, I wanted my husband to come home to a beautiful, clean home. I was so excited for him to see all of the changes I had made! I even had several friends who helped me do some (small) renovations, and it was a lot of fun, too.

Find something you can do during the deployment. Set some goals and try to accomplish them during the deployment or before the deployment ends. It could be a weight loss goal or trying a new hobby. Just picture how happy your spouse will be when he sees you have reached your goals, whatever they may be!

10. Pray some more.

This one is so important that I had to mention it again. Seriously, if you are currently going through a deployment, get on your knees right now and pray. I am speaking to myself here, too. I don't pray nearly as much as I should, and I know that really is the key to getting through each day.

One of the hardest parts of a military spouse's day can be bedtime – at least it was for me. It's quiet, you're alone, and your mind can wander, from the stress of the day, wondering if your husband is okay, or just worries about being alone in the house at night with all the creaks and strange noises.

It's no fun sleeping alone at night, but there are lots of things you can do to relax and help yourself fall asleep faster!

Ten Ways to Relax at Bedtime

1. Take a warm shower or bath.

I don't know about you, but I love a good, hot shower! I hop in the shower sometimes when I am upset and I let the water wash over me while I think, pray or cry. The warm water is good for your body and helps you to wind down and relax. I suggest 10 minutes at the very least before bed.

2. Read the Bible.

Even if you have already done your devotions for the day, read a passage of Scripture. I usually choose to read in Psalms or Proverbs because the verses in those books are very encouraging and make me feel better. Look up verses on sleep, fear, or peace. I guarantee after a few minutes of reading and studying, you will feel better about going to sleep alone. Here are a few verses to get you started:

> *"I will both lie down in peace, and sleep; for you alone, O Lord, make me dwell in safety."* – *Psalm 4:8* (NKJV)

> *"When you lie down, you will not be afraid; yes, you will lie down and your sleep will be sweet."* – *Proverbs 3:24* (NKJV)

Claim these verses and recite them to yourself before you go to sleep at night.

3. Read a book.

I don't know about you, but I can get lost in a good book from time to time–especially a good fiction book! Fiction has the power to wrap your mind into a story and take your mind off of your troubles and to make you feel, just for a few minutes, like you are a part of the story. I know for me, even reading a few minutes of a story would help get my mind off something I was worried about. It helped me relax more and gave me something to think about before I drifted off to sleep.

4. Listen to music.

Music can calm the soul and depending on the type of music it is, it can definitely relax you! Try listening to classical music, worship music, hymns, or spa music. Find something that works for you. I know at certain times when I've been afraid, I have fallen asleep with music I left on all night long. It was quiet enough to hear my son if he cried, but loud enough to make me relax and feel at peace. *Scripture Lullabies* released two CDs that are absolutely beautiful and perfect for relaxing and listening to at night.

5. Pray.

This one is kind of a given, but if you are unable to sleep, then pray. If you are afraid to sleep alone at night, then pray. Prayer works and it's the best way to get peace in your heart. It kind of sounds funny to say, but praying helps me fall asleep. I will usually lie in bed and pray until I fall asleep. If you can't think of anything to pray for, list things you are thankful for or list all the attributes of God you can think of.

6. Write your husband a letter.

Another thing I liked doing before bed was writing a letter or e-mail to my husband about my day or about whatever was on my mind. If it's not something you want to share with your husband at the moment, try journaling about it instead.

7. Listen to the rain.

A while back, someone on Twitter posted a link to a site that plays the sound of rain 24 hours a day. Since then, I have used it multiple times – especially while my husband was gone to help me sleep better. It is peaceful, relaxing, and it gave me something to listen to other than the strange creaking noises of our home. Just go to *RainyMood.com* and it will immediately start playing sounds of rain. I have left my computer on all night so I could listen to it while I slept. You can also download apps to your phone that do the same thing.

8. Breathe.

I have talked about this one before, but breathing is a great technique for relaxing your body. If done right, it can help you sleep better. I learned a lot about breathing in yoga, but one way you can practice breathing is to lay flat on your back and take a deep breath in and hold it. After holding it for a count of three, push out your breath slowly until it's all out. Repeat as many times as you want.

Another way to relax is to again lay flat on your back. Shake out your legs and arms a little bit and then relax all your muscles. Start at your toes and work your way up relaxing the muscles in each part of your body and concentrate on breathing in and out. Keep working your way up even to your head and neck. Relax the muscles in your face and mouth.

If you do it right, you should be very relaxed and maybe almost asleep by the time you are done!

9. Be prepared.

For me, it helped to have some sort of a plan of what would happen should someone break in, or if there was a tornado. Sure, it probably wasn't very likely, but it helped me feel better. I always made sure my doors were locked at night and I always slept with my husband's huge metal flashlight. I figured if the power went out, I would have the light, and if someone broke in, I would use it on their head. I know it's silly, but it made me feel better every night feeling that flashlight right next to me knowing I had a plan and I was a little prepared. Figure out what works for you and what makes you feel safe.

10. Don't force yourself.

If there was anything I learned about trying to sleep during deployment, it was to not push it. If you can't sleep, then don't force it. Try any of the suggestions above or just get up and get some stuff done until you are sleepy.

Asking for Help During Deployment

Another important key to making it through deployment is learning to ask for help. Over the years, I have spoken with many military wives who during their husband's deployment made clear their reluctance to ask for help if they needed it. They felt as though they would be a bother or annoying if they asked their friends to help with the kids, to drive them somewhere, or to help them with some minor chore.

I have wondered to myself why this is because I know there have been times where I would have dropped everything to help a friend in need, if I had only known what they were going through or that they needed help. That is even truer now that I have been through a deployment and multiple separations and know what it is like.

As military spouses I think we equate asking for help with not being strong, which is a lie Satan wants us to believe. There is nothing wrong with asking for help; it is only our pride that holds us back. I am not saying that I am perfect in this, because I am far from it and I always fear asking for help because I am afraid of what people will think. Will they wonder why I can't do it myself? Will they say yes only because they feel they have to? Will I feel stupid asking for help? These are just a few of the questions that have crossed my mind.

What holds us back from asking for help? The answer is fear and pride: fear of not being strong enough and pride that we can do it all ourselves, that we are "superwomen." That is not true. God did not create us to be like the Energizer Bunny, to keep on going and going and going. He created us to have rest sometimes, too. Even God rested. Genesis 2:2 says, *"And on the seventh day God ended his work which he had done, and he rested on the seventh day from all his work which he had done."* (NKJV)

I recently read an article on FaithDeployed.com called, *"Fake It Until You Make It."* It was about a military spouse who needed assistance to get through some things, but never asked for help. One thing led to the next, and now she is suffering long-term physical consequences. It saddened me, and I kept thinking, If only she had asked for help!

Please don't suffer in silence; ask for help if you need it. God gave you friends who love you and want to help bless you in your time of need, and he gave you a home church so that you could have encouragement and be lifted up. Use these people in your life; God has put them there for a reason!

Vanessa, an Army wife, says, "I learned during our first deployment to accept help. I had a neighbor offer to bring us a meal once a week and I felt weird accepting it. We weren't destitute and I wasn't bedridden (even though I was pregnant), so I didn't feel as though I needed any help with meals. Well, this neighbor told me that she wanted to do this for me and was persistent about it (in a nice way). She wanted to serve us and said that we were robbing her of God's blessings and that she wouldn't have offered the meal if she didn't want to do it. She wanted to help support the troops and this was the best way she could think of doing so.

The simple act of bringing us a meal freed me up for the night to spend time with my kids and not worry about cooking. In turn, my neighbor got the satisfaction of 'doing her part' in helping support the military. Over the past 10 years, I have learned that if someone offers to help me, I need to swallow my pride and accept that help. By accepting help, I may be doing my part in letting someone receive blessings from God that He wants to give them. This small act of kindness on her part ended up being a huge help to me and I was also blessed to know that people do care about us while our loved ones are deployed.

There will come a time in my life that I can be the giver and I think I need to remember that more often. Yes, I feel like I take a lot right now and never have an opportunity to give back, which is so against my character, but God is working in me, too. I'm learning to be gracious and to accept these small acts of kindness from others. God will provide a time in our lives for us to have an opportunity to be on the other side and be the giver rather than the receiver."

Chapter 10:
DEAR CIVILIANS

One time I had a conversation with someone at my church about my husband's deployment.

Her: How are you doing?

Me: I'm okay.

Her: Well, your husband comes home soon, right?

Me: No, he just left a month ago.

Her: Well, he'll be home by Christmas, right?

Me: No, you must be thinking of someone else.

Her: When does he get home then?

Me: (I told her what month.)

Her: WHAT? I thought the President said all the troops would be home by Christmas!

Me: (In shock) No, that is just for those in Iraq. There are tons of other troops in Afghanistan and all over the world.

We know that sometimes it's hard for civilians to understand military life and that sometimes their words can be hurtful or shocking. Before I was a military spouse, I had no idea what it was like. I didn't know much about the war, what was going on, and I knew absolutely nothing about military life. After my husband (then fiancé) joined the military, I soon discovered a whole new world – a world that people seem to forget about if they do not watch the news or read the papers. Not only do people not consider what current military families go through on a daily basis, but we also forget about those military families in the past during other wars that helped give our country the freedoms we have today.

Being a military spouse has made me so much more patriotic. It has made me more aware of the freedoms we have, why we have them, and the sacrifices that have been made by others so we could keep them. My goal since becoming a military spouse has been to encourage other military spouses, but it has also been to let people know what these families, these wonderful military families, go through every day.

This chapter is just for that! If you have family or friends who would like a little peek into what you go through and how they can help you, then have them read this chapter. I hope that by the end they will have a better understanding and that you, too, will benefit in knowing how to help other military families.

What Every Military Spouse Wants You to Know

People asked me, "How can I help?" or "What can we do?" while my husband was deployed. We appreciate you asking, but don't let not knowing what to do, or not understanding what military life is like, keep you from being there for a military spouse or loving on a military family!

Below is a list of questions asked by my very good civilian friend. She came to me asking these questions so she could know what it was like to be a military family and what she could do to help. I hope this helps others see that while we love our lives, they can sometimes be difficult and unique.

1. What kind of support could friends offer your husband or his troop? Group? I'm totally clueless as to what they are called...

In the Air Force, it is called a squadron. It may be different in other branches. And actually it just so happens that my husband's squadron does not deploy as a unit. If you sent something, it would be per person, not per squadron. If there was some kind of support you wanted to offer a deployed military member, I would suggest sending care packages, letters, and e-mails. Cookies are very much appreciated! Depending on who you are sending it to, you could ask their spouse or family what things they might need or like, such as snacks and toiletry items.

2. If I lived close to you, what would be the biggest help and support I could give to you?

I know a lot of civilian friends who feel the same way. They want to help, but they just aren't sure how to, and while a blanketed statement such as, "If you need anything, let me know," or "Let me know what I can do to help," is nice, it is sometimes embarrassing for us to have to ask. We don't want people to think we can't handle ourselves and our family while our husband is away.

Things you can do without asking:

- Do the yard work. Things such as mowing the lawn, raking, or shoveling are very helpful.

- Invite the family over. On a weekend(s), invite the family over for dinner or game night. Weekends are the hardest days of the week for military families because that is usually the time we would spend together as a family or on a date night with our spouses.

- Babysit. Don't ask them to tell you when they need you. Say that you would like to help out or give them a break once a week or month and have them pick a specific day.

- Invite them over on special days or holidays. Days such as their birthday and anniversary, and holidays such as Christmas, Thanksgiving, Easter, and the Fourth of July, are hard for military families while the spouse is gone. Invite them over or make sure they will not be alone on those days.

- Sit with them at church. If you go to church together, ask them to sit with your family so they do not have to sit alone.

- Do their grocery shopping. Offer to pick up groceries for them. They can always pay you back when you drop them off.

- Bring a meal over. Sometimes having a night off from the cooking is just the break the spouse needs!

- Don't just ask them how they are doing. They will most likely say, "I'm fine." Chances are that they are not. Instead, tell them hi, give them a hug, and tell them that you care about them and are praying for them. Then pray for them.

- Listen. Military spouses need a friend to vent to and talk to since it's just them and the children all day long. They will appreciate the listening ear when you offer it.

If you were to ask me which ones were the most important to me from this list, I would say babysitting and providing meals.

I can't tell you how many times I needed a sitter because of the doctor's appointments I had for all my health problems or because I just wanted a break to go out with a friend, but sometimes I couldn't afford to pay someone. EVERY single military spouse needs a break. Most are home all day alone with the kids and don't have any help. Having someone help watch the kids just so they can clean the house or be alone for a few minutes is more helpful than you would think.

Also, military spouses don't really see the point of cooking often while their spouse is gone. Of course we make food for the kids, but it's usually something easy. In my case, because my son has feeding problems, we eat at separate times and I make food just for me. I would usually just buy the frozen food dishes because it was so much easier than making a whole meal and cleaning up all of the dirty dishes. I loved the times someone sent food home with me because then I didn't have to worry about what to cook or eat another frozen food dish again!

As Briana, a fellow military wife, says, "It's not too hard to think of things to do to help. Just think if you were on your own, what would YOU miss? What would be nice for YOU?"

3. How can friends who don't live near you help and support you from afar? There have been several times that I've seen something that made me think of you, but I didn't know if it would be weird to send you little gifts or cards to brighten your day while your husband is away...

That is not weird at all! Some people think that care packages just apply to the military members, but you can also send them to military spouses and their families. I know that it would help cheer me up, encourage me, and make me feel loved, too.

Here are a few other things you can do:

- Check in and see how the spouse is doing on a regular basis.
- Be available to talk and chat. Sometimes they just want another adult to talk or vent to.
- Pray for and with them.
- Go visit them! If it's possible and if the family is up for it, go and stay with them for a week or two or invite them to your place for a mini-vacation.

4. What about your son? How is he taking his dad being away? Is there anything a friend could do for him? If not your son specifically, do you know of common needs of the children of people who have been deployed?

All military children are affected by deployment,

but depending on their age, it's sometimes harder to recognize. My husband left when my son was 16 months old and honestly, I don't think he really understood what was happening. He kind of just went on with life. I did sometimes see little things that let me know he still loved and missed his dad. He was excited when we Skyped, he would wave and blow kisses to his dad, and he went around saying, "Da-da-da" a lot.

But even at his young age, there is a lot someone could do to make things easier for him, such as:

- Have play dates. I found that the times he was playing with other kids were his happiest. Having people who were willing to do play dates with us and understanding behavior problems that might come up because Daddy was gone was a must.

- Be a "big brother." While my husband was gone, Adam still needed that male attention. Someone who was a little older –an adult, teenager, or big kid – who was willing to wrestle with him, have fun, get down in the dirt and do "boy stuff" was perfect and very helpful while he was missing his dad.

- Give them special attention and a little TLC. I'm not saying he needed to be spoiled because his dad was gone, but people letting him know that he was still loved and giving him a little extra attention was helpful so that he did not feel left out.

Aprille, a military spouse, says, "Honestly when you have little babies who are unaware of Daddy/Mommy being gone, the thing they need the most is a sane, loving, and relaxed Mommy/Daddy at home. I would just reiterate the need for the spouse at home to have a break – and lots of TLC!"

5. Okay, I am one that always puts my foot in my mouth, so what are some cliché sayings that people say to you that just get under your skin?

Oh, yes! We military spouses have a long list of them and we more than appreciate you asking. Here are just a few:

- "I could never do it!"
- "Do you miss them?"
- "What if they die?"
- "How do you do it?"
- "I know how you feel. My spouse has to go away on business trips sometimes, too." (Honestly, there is a huge difference between a deployment and someone going away on a business trip.)
- "I thought the war in Iraq was over!"
- "I thought you made a lot of money." (Actually, military members are paid very little.)
- "Well, you knew what you signed up for." (That may be true, but that doesn't mean it isn't hard and that we don't need help.)
- "Why can't they come home for Christmas / anniversary / birthday / birth of a child / wedding / family reunion / death?" (When a military member is deployed, they are not allowed to just drop everything and run home. Only in matters of emergency – life or death – can they come home. And even then, sometimes they will not be able to. It just depends on the situation and where they are at the time.)

- "Don't you miss sex? I couldn't do it!"

- "How long are they going to be gone? Oh...that's not bad." (I'm sorry, but gone is gone. None of it is fun.)

- If you want the explanation for some of these and why we don't appreciate these sayings, check out this article online: *What Not to Say to a Military Wife.*

- Also, please don't pity us or give us looks of pity. Military spouses do not want to be pitied; they want to be loved, cared about, and prayed for.

6. What is something that people don't say enough?

- "How are you?" (But really care and want to listen to how we are doing.)

- "I'm here for you."

- "Would you like to come over for dinner?"

- "Do you have someone helping with the lawn work?"

- "Would you like to go do something this weekend or hang out today?"

- "Do you have somewhere to go to for the holidays?" (And if not, invite them over that day!)

Military spouses speak out:

"For me, actions speak louder than words. Instead of making a general, 'I'm here if you need anything,' volunteer to do SPECIFIC things." – *Kayla*

"THANK YOU! In the six years that my husband has been in the service, I think he's only been told 'thanks' like five or six times." – *Stephanie*

"It's not that people don't say these things enough; it's that their words are rarely backed by action." – *Danielle*

"I wish people would say, 'I care. It matters. What he does is important,' and truly MEAN it. I sometimes feel they say what they do because it's in context of the conversation. Almost obligatory." – *Erin*

7. If you could tell us civilians one thing to help us understand what it's like to be in your shoes during deployment, what would it be?

It is the hardest and scariest thing I have ever done. And while that really is the case, it is also a learning and growing process. We love our husbands and we support them. Even though it's hard, we are still blessed.

Other military spouse answers:

"We don't go through deployments because we want to. We survive them because we have to." – *Lauren*

"Sometimes you just have to hide behind smiles and pretend nothing is wrong." – *Kaitlin*

"Being in the shoes of a spouse of a deployed service member is like wearing shoes that don't quite fit, but they were too cute to pass on. You wear them day in and day out because they go with everything, but each step pinches just a little bit and feels off. I love my husband and can't imagine life without him, but each day during a deployment stings no matter how great it is because he's not with me." – *Becky*

"I know you can't understand, but for once, stop saying that you don't or can't understand and just TRY." – *Aprille*

"Sometimes being a soldier isn't what he does, but it's who he is. You don't have to understand that to be our support. You just need to be our friend." – *Kim*

8. Do you think the average military spouse has the support and love they need from their friends and family while their spouse is away?

After polling tons of military spouses through Facebook, I have come to the conclusion that it's about 50-50. It depends on the type of family they have, where they are stationed, if they just moved to that state or if they have been there for a while, if they have a church family, and if they have good neighbors. However, almost every single person said that other military spouses are their best support, not civilians. This is mostly because another military spouse is going to understand much better what we are going through.

Military spouses speak about their support systems:

"It kind of depends, I think. I know some military spouses are very 'connected' in terms of having lots of supportive family and friends who understand. I really battle with feeling alone even though I have support. I am a National Guard wife living hours away from my husband's unit, and I don't know any military spouses here." – *Rebekah*

"If they are a military spouse, then yes, I would say so for the most part. But ONLY if you put yourself out there to FIND a support system. For me, all of my family and friends are civilians and they have no clue nor do they care about the things they could do to ease a deployment." – *Lauren*

"From their family? I would say no. I know I don't because we are the only military in my family so no one else understands. From my friends, yes and no.

I have some military friends, but my civilian friends don't understand at all." – *Stephanie*

"My immediate family and military friends are [my support system]. Civilian friends, not so much, which is why I have very few of them!" – *Aprille*

"No, I feel like our credit is lost! We become Mom and Dad all while our spouse is away and we are almost living a single life. There's a lot more emotionally involved in all of this that takes place. Not to mention, the simple task of shopping takes three times as long. My family is great and they all understand what I'm going through and help out amazingly. But that's not the case for everyone." – *McKenzie*

"I know that a lot of civilian friends really don't get it, but when my husband was gone for two months I only had civilian friends. Even though they didn't understand what I was going through, they tried and they really helped me out. It was good to at least have someone that was willing to be there for me whether they got it or not." – *Jessica*

"I would say that before I met my husband, I had no idea what military families went through. I was almost oblivious to it, especially since my family growing up had no one enlisted and we never talked about it much. But once I married my husband and went through three long deployments, I definitely approached military families differently and tried to help them out and support them as much as I could! I had a lot of support from my family and friends, but the most came from those who actually went through deployments before. The best thing (besides prayer of course!) was just venting or talking with the military spouses who became like family to me. I tried also not to get upset at those who didn't call enough or try to help out enough, because sometimes people are just oblivious and don't understand what we go through as military spouses." – *Sarah*

9. If you do not have that love and support, what is the MAIN thing that is missing from your life, or from the lives of others you have seen that a friend could provide?

Every military spouse is different, but for me, I am not very independent. I don't like to be alone. I would love to have someone to talk to most of the time or to hang out with. I think the main thing is to just be there for them and to listen or to hear them cry and vent, even if you don't understand what they are going through.

10. This is one I always feel awkward about. I don't know how often you get to talk to your spouse, so should we ask how they are doing? Or when you talked last? Or let you bring it up when you want to?

Yes, please do ask how they are doing! I have felt sad in the past when I have gone to parties, church functions, or other events and not a single person asked how my husband was doing. It made me feel like no one cared, even though I am sure they did, and they just didn't think about asking. You can ask when we last talked, but just know that every deployment is different. Sometimes we get to talk a lot and other times we may not get to talk very much at all.

Keep in mind that if you ask about specific dates or when they are coming home, we may not be able to talk about it. There are rules called **OPSEC** that sometimes don't permit us to say things, especially online. Also, homecoming dates tend to change a lot and never stay the same, so while you might want to ask, keep in mind they might not even know when your spouse is coming home, or they might know, but it could change again later.

11. What is the best thing someone has done for you during your spouse's deployment?

Throughout our first deployment there was one person (and her family) who was always there for me, and I honestly don't know what I would have done without them. The Russell family (also a military family) became my greatest support system and Michelle Russell was the one person I went to, to ask questions, cry to, vent to, and get advice.

They invited my son and me over for lunch almost every Sunday that my husband was away, they invited me to sit with them in church so I didn't have to sit alone, and their sons took time to play with Adam and make him laugh. Their daughter, Emily, babysat Adam on almost a weekly basis and sometimes several times a week. Sometimes, she even did it for free. They once even let me borrow their car for a few days when I had car trouble.

For the first several months during the deployment they watched my son for free so I could go to a yoga class on base. They told me they wanted me to have some time for myself and they wanted to do it for free to bless me. Michelle went to the hospital with me, gave me advice, talked me through my son getting sick at three in the morning, prayed with me, drove a total of six hours with me to see a specialist, and listened as I cried and cried when my husband's grandfather died. Ed Russell helped to fix my car, my vacuum, and even my internet connection! He also gave my son haircuts for me. I can't even begin to say what a blessing they were to me. We need more people like that in this world!

Dear Civilians: What You Need to Know About Military Homecomings and Reintegration

Reintegration is the period of time that happens after a military member comes home from deployment. It's the time where the member and the family learn about becoming a family again after being apart for so long. It can be a difficult time depending on the family and how many times they have been through a deployment. While my family's reintegration went much better than I had hoped, it is not always the same for other military families. This is a time for you to pray for them and check in on them to see how they are doing.

Homecoming is an event that military families everywhere hope for, dream of, and look forward to. But homecoming is not what everyone thinks it is. It is not always the fairytale that television shows and movies make it out to be. Homecoming is hard, and it's definitely not always happily ever after.

My friend, Aprille, has been through several deployments and several tough reintegration periods. She wrote this next part of the chapter from her experiences in hopes that it will help civilians understand better what we as military families go through after a long deployment.

Military reunions are portrayed as very exciting and happy experiences, but what a lot of people don't realize is that homecoming and reintegration are very difficult times as well. For a military family, the weeks before their reunion is an anxiety-filled wait, and the weeks and months after their reunion are filled with many challenges.

"No, I don't know when he is coming home!"

"So when is he coming home?" This is probably the most frequently asked question a military spouse receives. Naturally, others are excited for them because they are finally going to be reunited with their spouse! But for the soldier who is traveling home from the other side of the world, it's a complicated multi-step process. There are chopper and plane schedules, other military personnel who may need to rush home for emergencies, weather factors, and of course, the presence of the enemy and the battles of the war.

For this reason, homecoming details are never finalized until the last minute, change often, and need to be kept very secret to keep our military members safe. The earliest notice I have ever received of exactly when my husband was arriving home was 14 hours, and even then, his flight ended up landing two hours later than expected. The military projects estimates and approximates to the families for planning purposes, but those estimates are rarely exactly when it actually ends up happening.

For the spouse who loves and supports their service member, the process is just as frantic. There are chores to get done, banners to make, balloons to blow up, middle of the night phone calls to answer, hopes and dreams about the return to deal with, and the fear of what problems or stresses the soldier might be bringing home with them. The bottom line is that homecoming is not just this dreamy "wish come true" in which everyone lives happily ever after. Even at its best, it's a challenge and a struggle for all parties involved.

The World English Dictionary defines "reintegrate" as "to make or be made into a whole again." Deployments split military families into fragments, and the process of putting those fragments back together and making the family whole again is difficult and painstaking. With that in mind, here are some things that friends and family can do to support a military family experiencing a reunion after deployment.

Please respect our homecoming wishes.

Some military members will want all their extended family there to welcome them home from war; others only want their spouses (even leaving the children with a sitter). This will depend on the personality of the service member and the dynamics of his or her family. If we ask you not to attend the ceremony or come into town for homecoming, PLEASE understand that this is not some sort of personal attack on you. We just need some space and alone time to get used to each other again before adding the stress of extended family and friends. If we ask you to come, then come, but understand that we will still need space. Make hotel accommodations and don't plan big surprises or parties for that week. The greatest need a returning service member has the first week he or she is home is sleep and peace.

*Not everyone has the same
homecoming experience.*

Every family's personality is different. Some couples will run to each other, jump into each other's arms, cry and kiss and hug for a long time before leaving the homecoming facilities. Others, like my husband and I, favor a quick peck on the cheek and "let's just get out of here" approach and save the more intimate and emotional reunion for the privacy of our own homes. Neither is right or wrong. And while we may imagine or plan it a certain way, when that moment actually happens, it rarely ends up going the way we envisioned it. Please don't put expectations on us as to how we should or should not act at homecoming.

"There are no unwounded soldiers!"

No service member comes back from a deployment without bearing some scars of what they have experienced. It doesn't matter if they were in Iraq, Kuwait, Africa, or Afghanistan, if they sat at a desk or behind a sniper rifle, or if they were gone for six weeks or 16 months. Will there be varying degrees of their wounds? Absolutely. But ALL will be affected in some way. Soldiers experience long work hours, no breaks, monotony, lack of American comforts, fatigue, adjusting their bodies to a new time zone (and then back again), anxiety, sleep disorders, fear, sinful temptations, and time spent away from their precious families. Nothing about deployment is enjoyable or easy.

Please don't downplay a service member's wounds because they are "invisible" or because the soldier "seems fine." You have no idea what they have been through or what they and their families now have to deal with for the rest of their lives. Even little things like stuttering or being uncomfortable in social situations can be little symptoms of the "invisible wounds" they are trying to heal. Please don't mock these things or take them personally.

Every military spouse is now a caretaker.

As the service member begins to heal from their physical and invisible wounds, the primary person who steps in to care for them during that process is the spouse. For some spouses, this means attending multiple appointments, sitting beside hospital beds, and driving their service member everywhere they need to go. For others, the responsibilities are less consuming, but still include being a calming presence in stressful situations or providing comfort after nightmares and sleep disturbances.

Military spouses whose military members are facing problems like severe anxiety and PTSD can find themselves dealing with secondary or anticipatory anxiety and PTSD. Often, they get so used to their soldiers reacting in a certain way to stress, that in seeking to lessen their reactions, they anticipate the reactions ahead of time and develop their own anxiety about the upcoming situation. This stress can cause severe emotional and physical fatigue, which in time can make it harder and harder for them to care for the needs of their soldier. Look for ways to help alleviate the stress of a military spouse. Offer a quick hug, a prayer, or just a listening ear for when they get overwhelmed.

"Mommy/Daddy just needs a break!"

A military spouse getting ready to be reunited with their spouse, especially one who has small children, fantasizes about getting a break. They dream of the other parent taking over all of the responsibilities seamlessly while they finally get a chance to set down the burdens they have been carrying for the last few months: the burdens of being a single parent, taking out the trash every week, managing the home and finances, and staying up late for Skype dates and phone calls.

While some of this does in fact happen once the family is reunited, the service member's homecoming brings a whole new set of responsibilities to her plate. The service member may even be unable to step back into the roles that they were filling before they deployed for various reasons. So now the military spouse is caring for their spouse's wounds, adapting to their schedule, doing loads and loads of extra laundry, and actually having to cook real meals again (as opposed to eating ice cream for dinner!).

On top of the extra responsibilities, the military spouse's current responsibilities become more difficult. Children most often react to stress (even good stress) by acting out. They misbehave more, sleep and nap less, and are just out of sorts in general. They are adjusting to Daddy/Mommy being home again, but Daddy/Mommy is different than what they remembered. Sometimes the service member may be distant, moody, and angry, or they may even curse on accident. Small children cannot comprehend what has happened to Daddy/Mommy. They just know that things are different. Oh, and why does Daddy/Mommy suddenly want to take so much of the military spouse's attention? "No, she's MY Mommy!" "That's MY Daddy!" Toddlers can become jealous that they no longer have your undivided attention. And there's pretty much nothing worse to a service member with mental difficulties than a screaming baby! Suddenly, the-military-spouse-who-just-dreams-of-finally-getting-a-break begins to feel more like the rope used in the game of tug of war between the cranky kids and the stressed-out service member.

Over the two-week mid-tour leave during my husband's second deployment, and the weeks following his homecoming, the word I could have used most to describe how I felt was simply exhausted! Look for specific ways to lend a helping hand to the military spouse that you know. Offer to take their children for the evening so that the two of them can have a quiet evening at home to themselves. Offer to bring them a meal.

If you have been providing services like lawn care, taking out the trash, or car maintenance, ask them if they would like you to continue while their spouse adjusts to simply being home. Provide social outlets for them by continuing to invite them over for coffee dates or girl's/guy's nights out. While at first we military spouses love to spend every waking moment with our returned service member, after a week or two we start to go through "friend withdrawal" and sometimes a heart-to-heart talk with a friend provides just the perspective we need to hold ourselves together for one more draining day.

Reintegration is just hard.

One of the best illustrations I can think of to explain what reintegration is like is that of first-time parents bringing home their newborn. Those first few weeks are both blissful and brutal! Yes, they are so glad that the misery of pregnancy is FINALLY over, but now they have to deal with a lack of sleep, trying to get into a new routine, grieving the loss of a carefree we-can-do-whatever-we-want-when-we-want   marriage, and a ton of extra responsibilities. Being a new parent is just hard!

We as military spouses would no more send our spouses back to war than new parents would take that wonderful new baby back to the hospital. Of course, we are incredibly thankful to God that the misery of deployment is finally over and, yes, we are thankful that our spouses are home safely! But that doesn't mean it's all blissful, easy, and wonderful either. If you see us in the store and we seem like we are acting less-than-in-love and snapping at our children, it doesn't mean that we are headed for divorce; it may just mean that Daddy/Mommy had a nightmare which woke up the baby and then neither Daddy/Mommy nor baby could go back to sleep and the military spouse was a ping-pong ball between them all night. Everyone is just exhausted! Please don't pass critical judgments on us if we aren't blissfully happy all the time.

Reintegration takes as long as it takes.

How long does it take to make a family "whole" again? According to the National Association of School Psychologists, "Successful reintegration does not happen overnight; it takes time (as long as seven months)..." Army Chaplain Thomas W. Cox spoke at a briefing on combat stress hosted by Operation Faithful Support and stated that it can actually take as long as 18 months. The truth is that the answer will differ from family to family, from service member to service member.

This process is further complicated by multiple and recurring deployments. My husband found out less than three months after he returned home from his first deployment that his unit was scheduled to deploy again the following year. At that point, "reintegration" (trying to make our family whole) became just a dread-filled break from another deployment. There are things that we did not deal with properly because we were just anticipating being ripped apart again, so what was the point? (In hindsight, that was the wrong attitude to have, but this is a very natural response among military families.)

Often, the service member is home just a few months before he has to uproot his struggling-to-reintegrate family off to another duty station to face more training for yet another deployment in the months ahead. I have another friend whose husband is an Air Force pilot who deploys on a three-months-home then three-months-deployed schedule. It makes for quite an emotional roller coaster for the family. The military doesn't make it exceptionally easy for military families to reintegrate because they rarely have enough time to do so fully. In many a case, a family is never completely made whole again. Just as a shattered vase will still have cracks and scrapes even when glued back together, most military families bear the scars of multiple separations and deployments, and are just held together by faith, love, and the grace of God.

Above all, pray for patience and healing for all military families. Be patient with them. If you are loving and supporting a military family facing a reunion and reintegration, know that you are in this journey with them for the long haul. Don't "jump off the wagon" when it gets hard. Stay by them, love them, and support them without judgment even when they seem less-than-pleasant or become distant when they face difficulties.

Not every military family will face all of the challenges described here. Some families reintegrate smoothly; others have a much harder time. Remember that every military family is different. But what we all have in common is that we need love, understanding, patience, and prayer.

Chapter 11:
END OF DEPLOYMENT BLUES

I'm going to be honest. The last few months of our first deployment were hard. Things were quiet at home – almost too quiet after all the Murphy's Law catastrophes we had during most of that deployment. But as we neared the end, I felt tired and done. I didn't want to think anymore and I didn't want to do anything. I just wanted my husband home.

I didn't realize that all the feelings I had felt in the beginning of deployment would circle around to the end, but they did. Sometimes it felt like I had been punched in the stomach, like, "Whoa, this is really happening," and "Whoa, look what I've gotten through," and "Whoa, it still feels like an eternity until he comes home."

One Sunday night on the way to church, I started thinking about the homecoming. I pictured myself at the airport waiting at the gate. I was in the homecoming dress I had already picked out, and I stood at the window watching his plane come in. Just thinking about it made the tears start to fall. All the feelings of everything that had happened during the deployment began to flood me, and in my mind I could just feel the relief I knew would come the second my eyes met his.

Sometimes I would wonder if I was going crazy. I finally understood why some people call military life a roller coaster. The ups and downs of feelings and emotions can be crazy. It IS crazy. And the roller coaster of emotions I felt was just the beginning!

Some days I was fine and happy, and other days I wanted him home so bad I could have screamed. Sometimes when I was lying there in bed, I would just picture our homecoming over and over and over in my head. The airport, the pictures, the hug and kiss, and then going home together. The airport, the pictures, the hug and kiss, and then going home together. Over and over and over again I pictured him home again, in our house again, holding his hand again, and watching him play with our son again.

I wondered, Did he change? Have I changed? Will our marriage be different? Will we pick back up where we left off? Sure, it wouldn't be easy – I knew that. But I couldn't help but picture all of these things, think about them, and imagine how they would turn out.

I would wake up each day and think, Oh, yeah, another long day of staying home and doing nothing, and then I would think of how I just had to get out of the house. I found things to do to keep me busy so my mind didn't explode. But at night when I was home and it was quiet, it was all I could think about. Sometimes I couldn't even sleep. And when I did sleep, all I did was dream about it.

Sometimes I felt the energy and the anxiety coursing through me; it made me feel like if I didn't immediately get up and do something, I was going to go crazy. I put my energy into exercising or taking my son to the park or cleaning the house – anything to keep my mind off how many days and weeks we had left.

These feelings I had at the end of deployment are normal! The anxiety, anticipation, and the waiting are enough to make anyone crazy, but take heart: your lists will get done, your life will settle back down once your spouse is home again, and the calm and peace you crave right now will come again.

During this time, God sent me several "love letters" –things that showed me He was still there walking me through this to the very end. It was as if He was saying, "Why are you so worried and stressed? I am here; you have nothing to worry about."

One of these love letters was an email I received from a young woman who had recently found my blog. She had sent me a message to tell me she has been praying for God to send her a military spouse to encourage. As soon as I read that, tears were rolling down my face. The email had come just after I had been praying about how discouraged I was about the deployment. This email was like a letter sent from God to let me know how much He loved me and cared for me and how He was really listening to my prayers.

This particular love letter and the other ones He sent to me were so eye-opening. I think if you look for them, you will see them, too. Maybe throughout your deployment you have been put through so much. Test after test and hardship after hardship. God may be using these things to help you grow and to become a better, stronger person.

As our deployment neared its end, things calmed down for me and God showed me that even through the hardships of deployment, He still loved me. He was taking care of me the whole time and He had never forgotten about me or not known what was going on. He allowed all the catastrophes that happened to happen for a reason, and I saw this as I looked back on everything. I hope that you are able to see it, too.

Post-Deployment

Chapter 12:
HOMECOMING

You hear the stories, watch the television shows, and see the photos, but nothing prepares you for your very own homecoming! The weeks leading up to it are filled with anxiety, nervousness, and excitement. The days leading up to it are even worse. This is my homecoming story.

It took everything I had to keep busy. I filled my schedule up wherever I could and finally, as our homecoming date got closer, I started getting excited. I realized this was really going to happen – my husband was really coming home! During this time I pictured what it was going to be like. Would everything be the same as before? Would homecoming be awkward or would I run to him not caring who was watching?

The last word I heard before my husband got on his plane headed for home, was that he would be arriving in the United States early on a Sunday night.

I was shocked because we weren't expecting him until Monday or Tuesday. I didn't want to get my hopes up too much, but I was very excited. All day Sunday I was so antsy. I watched the clock waiting for 8 p.m. to arrive, the time he told me he would arrive in the United States.

Finally, I got the phone call. He had arrived safely in the United States and I was so relieved. It was an incredible feeling. Now all he had to do was find a flight home that night. He told me he would call me back and let me know. I was so excited and was praying my heart out he could get a flight that night.

While I waited, I had to make a ton of phone calls. I had a photographer coming with me so I needed to let her know what was going on so she could get a sitter for her kids, and I had to call my two babysitters I had lined up to find out who could watch my son. I was going crazy waiting for him to call back. After about 40 minutes, he called and said the ticket counter was closed until morning and there were no more flights out. I was really disappointed, but I knew this could happen. One more night wouldn't be too bad, I told myself.

He told me the ticket counter opened at 4 a.m. and he would be there to try to get the first flight out. I was still very excited. I called all the same people back, and made arrangements to call them in the morning when I knew what the plan would be. I made myself eat some dinner, and by that time I was so exhausted by the emotional roller coaster of everything that I went to bed.

At 5 a.m., I was woken up by a phone call. His flight was going to leave at 6:30 a.m. The flight took the same amount of time as it did for me to drive to the airport, which meant I had exactly 30 minutes to get ready, dressed, and get my son over to the sitter's house. It took me 45 minutes. Thankfully, I had already showered the night before, and so I just did my hair and makeup. I packed my son's things, woke him up and headed to my friend's house to drop him off and rush out the door.

By this time, I was running pretty late and was not even sure if I would make it to the airport on time to meet my husband's flight. The photographer, who was meeting me at the airport, and I had decided to try to meet him at the gate. She knew how to get a special pass for military spouses that allowed us to go and meet our husbands if they were coming back from a deployment. His flight was due sometime after 8 a.m. and it was going to be pretty close.

I was making some pretty awesome time getting to the airport – until I hit Atlanta. All the people who work in Atlanta were also trying to get into Atlanta. I was only a couple of miles from the airport and hit some very bad traffic. I was going crazy. I had about 20 minutes to get through traffic, park, get a pass, go through security, and get to the gate. Finally, after what seemed like forever, the traffic eased up and I arrived at the airport.

I parked, ran into the airport in my dress and high heels, ignoring the stares I was getting, and called my photographer. I couldn't find her anywhere and she was not answering her phone. I think I called her about 12 times. Finally she called me back and told me that she didn't think we could get passes to the gate. The line to get through security was a 35-minute wait. I was disappointed, but at this point his plane was going to be here anytime so I didn't care. I just wanted to see him.

We walked to the entrance where we knew he and all the other passengers would be coming through to get to baggage claim, and then the wait began. His flight was on time, but it seemed like it was arriving a little later then we had thought. I had to remind myself of how long it takes to park the plane and for all the passengers to get off.

He didn't have his phone with him, so I wasn't sure if he would be able to call me or not. Previously, he had borrowed other people's phones so he could give me a quick call to let me know what was going on. The waiting was killing me. I was so nervous; there were a couple times I thought I might throw up. I didn't know when he was going to come up over that escalator so all I could do was keep watching and waiting.

I checked my phone several times, but I had somehow still missed a phone call. I knew my husband had borrowed a phone but I wasn't sure if I should try calling that person back or just continue to wait. A few minutes later I got another phone call. It was a man on the other end telling me that my husband asked him to tell me that he is on his way to baggage claim, God bless me and to have a good reunion. I was touched. I was also shaking. Now he could be coming any minute. My eyes scanned the crowd just waiting to catch a glimpse of him.

From the second I saw my husband, everything else faded away. I could feel myself running (as best I could in high heels) the short distance to meet him and then it was over. The second we touched, our deployment was over and I could feel the relief fill my body. We hugged so tightly and he picked me up and I didn't give a second thought to what anyone else was doing. It was like for those few seconds we were the only ones left in the world.

We walked over to where our photographer was and he told me he had to go to the bathroom. I didn't want to ever let him go again, but I did. We hugged and kissed some more and then we went to get his baggage. I had a huge smile on my face. I felt complete again and there was nothing in the world that was going to bring me down in those moments.

Of course, we all know it doesn't end there. Life goes on, but that day will forever be etched into my memory. The weeks that followed were wonderful. I was worried about how reintegration would be and it definitely was not as bad as I had pictured. Being able to do everything together again, even to just hold hands, or sit next to each other or in the same room, was the most amazing feeling in the world. It taught me not to take a single day for granted. Homecoming: there's nothing like it.

No matter what, there is no wrong way to "do" homecoming. You can bring the kids or leave them home; you can get a photographer or have a private homecoming. No matter what you do it will be perfect for you and your spouse

Remember not to have too many expectations; be at peace with the day and that you are finally reunited with your loved one again. Enjoy it.

Chapter 13:
REINTEGRATION: PUTTING THE PIECES BACK TOGETHER

Once you experience homecoming, the journey is still not over. The reintegration period starts and for some families it can be a tough experience. My friend, Aprille, wrote this chapter and I hope it helps you as much as it helped me.

A military family that has gone through a deployment is much like a puzzle that has been wrecked and the pieces scrambled. After the deployment, the family has to put their puzzle back together. Here are some tips to help you through this process:

1. The puzzle you are putting back together is going to look different than it did before.

Your family will never be the same as it was, or function in the same way as it did before this separation.

Your "new normal" is going to look different from your "old normal."

2. Put the border together first.

Find all the straight pieces, the easy ones, the ones you know haven't changed. "We love each other. He's home safe. Nothing else matters." You might not feel "in love" or always see all the results of your love, but you have to know it's there. The rest of the pieces may be scattered – it might not look like you can EVER put it back together. But you still have the border, and that's a start!

3. Focus on connecting one piece at a time.

For us, it was simple things like holding hands or fixing my husband's coffee. It's small, but it's a connection. Little by little, the more connections you make, the closer you are to putting the whole puzzle back together.

4. Set aside the hard sections that you are struggling to connect and come back to them when you have more of the puzzle put together.

Remember that there is no "set time" to how quickly you should reintegrate. It takes time. Don't brush problems under the rug or ignore them completely, but recognize that not everything is going to connect easily and quickly.

5. Don't compare your puzzle to others.

The Smith's might only have 100 pieces in their puzzle while you have 1,000 in yours. Things like children, combat stress, unit casualties, pregnancy, or a new baby add pieces to the puzzle. The Smith's puzzle might look better than yours; you might even be able to see their whole picture when you can't see yours. But it doesn't matter. Focus on YOUR puzzle.

6. Don't be afraid to ask for help in putting your puzzle back together.

Puzzles usually get put together faster when there are more hands involved. Sometimes, you just need someone to ask, "Have you considered flipping this piece upside down? I think it would actually fit there!" Having objective help can be crucial in seeing the big picture. It is very rare that a military family would NOT need some sort of outside mediation to help them reintegrate. Please don't be too proud (or ashamed) to ask for help with the tough sections of your puzzle.

Above all, remember that you love each other and it doesn't have to be perfect. Give it time.

Chapter 14:
WHAT I LEARNED DURING DEPLOYMENT

Deployment was a huge learning process for me as I am sure it will be for you too. It changed me – not for worse like I thought it would, but for the better. Here are some things I learned from it and some things you might be able to learn, too!

1. I learned that I am stronger than I think.

No military spouse is ever ready for deployment. From what I hear from other spouses, none of us really feel that we are strong enough to go through a deployment. But at the end, when we look back, we are shocked at how much we came through and how strong we really are.

That is how it was with me. I look back and I think, *Wow, how did I do that?* The answer: I did it with God's help, and also by taking it one day at a time. There were a lot of days that I look back on when I felt I couldn't go on, but since I didn't have a choice in the matter, I kept on going. Those are the days that I believe make a person stronger. When you realize your only choice is to keep going, you do. When you finally look back, you realize how strong you really were, and how much of a stronger person you are now.

2. I learned that trusting God is my only option.

It's sad that it had to come down to a deployment to make me realize this. So many times I try to do things on my own and I don't think about trusting God or having faith in Him to do what He needs to do. At the beginning of the year I had picked the word "trust" for my theme for the year and something for me to work on. It's funny because when you actively ask God to help you learn how to trust, then He is definitely going to put things in your life to help you learn how to trust, and those things aren't always going to be what we think they are!

It was those times when I was at the end of my rope, when I felt like there just had to be something else I could do, that I heard that soft and still quiet voice that said, "Just trust." And that is what I learned: at the end of it all and even at the beginning, our only option is to trust. Because if we don't trust Him for the little things, then how can we trust Him for the big things in our lives?

3. I learned that letting others help me is necessary and that's okay.

If there is one thing I hear from military spouses the most, it's that they are afraid to let others help them during deployment. Either they are too proud to ask or they don't want others to think they are not strong enough to make it through the deployment on their own. For me it was a little of both.

During our deployment, it was pretty much impossible for me to get through without asking for at least a little help. And that's okay. It's okay to ask for help. In fact, I encourage you to do so if you are going through a deployment. Don't be afraid! A lot of military spouses see each other as family, and wouldn't you want to ask your family for help if you needed it? It took a wonderful woman at the beginning of this deployment who forced me to let her in and let her help, to get me to see this, and I am so glad I did.

4. I learned that deployment can be a time for personal growth.

During our first deployment I learned so much about myself. I grew as a person, I learned more about who I am, what I want, and a little about what makes me tick. If you are currently going through a deployment, use this time to better yourself and to learn about yourself. See what things in your life you can work on improving before your spouse gets home. It will be amazing to see the results at the end of the deployment!

5. I learned that deployment can make your marriage stronger.

At the beginning of our deployment, I was absolutely terrified of what it might do to our marriage. Would we change? Would our marriage change? Would we even know each other at the end of all this? Deployment is scary, and I think every deployment is different when it comes to your marriage.

It depends on what place you are at in your marriage when the deployment takes place. It also depends on what you make of it. Are you going to be an understanding spouse? Are you going to pray your way through? Are you going to have a positive outlook even when you both may not feel like it or when you are both having a bad day? Sure, there will be times you are going to argue, or be short with one another, but what I found more than that was that we were able to communicate our needs better.

We didn't have any real face-to-face conversations. We e-mailed. And when you e-mail, you have more time to respond. It gives each of you time to think through a response, and it also gives you a chance to write down your thoughts and feelings without getting interrupted.

At times, I felt the communication was slow and that was frustrating. But there were so many other times when I was able to really communicate how I felt about something through e-mail. This gave him time to think about it and then gave me time to respond instead of us interrupting each other or arguing about it.

Deployment CAN make a marriage stronger you just have to find a way to do it. Don't let it get you down; find ways to encourage and strengthen each other.

Conclusion

You have come to the end of this book and maybe even the end of your journey. I hope this book has been helpful to you and that your journey through deployment has been made a little easier from reading it.

Deployment is a tough journey and each one has its own unique facets. Learning to get through each one is a part of our lives as military spouses, and while it's definitely a unique journey, it certainly has its blessings, too. You just have to be willing to look for them.

A verse that has helped me through every trial and growing period in my life has been Deuteronomy 31:6 (NKJV), which says: *"Be strong and of a good courage, do not fear nor be afraid...for the Lord your God, he is the one who goes with you. He will not leave you or forsake you."* This was a verse I repeated to myself over and over during my husband's first deployment. It was what helped me get through each day. I hope that, like me, you can find a verse or even use this one to help you get through and finish your current deployment journey and the next ones that come along!

If you are looking for more encouragement and help for military life and deployment, you can find more encouraging posts on my blog at: SingingThroughTheRain.net.

Recommended Resources

Links:

Blue Star Families
www.bluestarfam.org

Daddy Dolls
www.daddydolls.com

Faith Deployed
www.faithdeployed.com

Give an Hour
www.giveanhour.org

Military Believer
www.militarybeliever.com

Military OneSource
www.militaryonesource.mil

National Military Family Association
www.militaryfamily.org

Operation We Are Here
www.operationwearehere.com

Operation Worship
www.operationworship.com

Operation: Love Reunited
www.oplove.org

Wives of Faith
www.wivesoffaith.org

Yellow Ribbon Churches
www.mnyellowribbonchurches.org

Books:

1001 Things to Love About Military Life by Tara Crooks

Closing The Gap: Understanding Your Service (wo)man by Yvonne Jones

Faith Deployed: Daily Encouragement for Military Wives by Jocelyn Green

Faith Deployed Again: More Daily Encouragement for Military Wives by Jocelyn Green

God Strong: The Military Wife's Spiritual Survival Guide by Sara Horn

Heroes at Home: Help and Hope for America's Military Families by Ellie Kay

Hope for the Home Front: Winning the Emotional and Spiritual Battles of a Military Wife by Marshele Carter Waddell

Hope for the Home Front Bible Study: Winning the Emotional and Spiritual Battles of a Military Wife by Marshele Carter Waddell

Military Wives' New Testament With Psalms & Proverbs: 90 Days of Encouragement and Hope by Jocelyn Green

Surviving Deployment: A Guide for Military Families by Karen M. Pavlicin

Tour of Duty: Preparing Our Hearts for Deployment by Sara Horn

For kids: *Countdown 'til Daddy Comes Home* by Kristin Ayyar

About The Author

Kathryn Sneed is a young Air Force spouse who has a passion for other military spouses. She served one year as a Key Spouse in her husband's squadron; helping military spouses in the unit get through deployments and checking in on them to see how they were doing. She also started an online group for the spouses at her base to ask questions, make friends, and get information about the area around the base as well as planning events that spouses could attend to meet and make new friends.

She started blogging seriously in 2009 and found that her blog was the perfect place to write about her experiences as a military spouse and to encourage other spouses going through similar situations.

In 2011, when her husband deployed, she realized the need was great for encouragement in the area of deployment and set to work blogging her way through that first deployment.

Since then, her posts have been featured on blogs from MilitaryConnection.com, FaithDeployed.com MilitaryFamily.com, SpouseLink.org and many other sites as she continues to encourage military families.

Kathryn currently resides at Robins Air Force Base in Georgia with her husband and two children. When she is not writing or blogging, she enjoys spending time with her family, going on date nights with her husband, making new friends, and reading a good book.

Connect with Kathryn on her blog:
SingingThroughTheRain.net

And find her online at

Facebook - www.facebook.com/
singingthroughtherain

Twitter - twitter.com/MyAFWifeLife

Pinterest - www.pinterest.com/kathrynann24/

Google+ - www.plus.google.com/+KathrynSneed

Instagram - www.instagram.com/
singingthroughtherain#

CPSIA information can be obtained
at www.ICGtesting.com
Printed in the USA
LVHW081328050319
609558LV00026B/279/P